Pre-K Math
Concepts from Global Sources

by Cynthia M. Manthey

HUMANICS™ LEARNING

P.O. Box 7400
Atlanta, GA 30357

Copyright © 1996 Humanics Limited. All rights reserved. No part of this book may be reproduced by any means, nor transmitted, nor translated into a machine language, without written permission from Humanics Limited.

Design and illustrations by Susan Chamberlain

PRINTED IN THE UNITED STATES OF AMERICA
Library of Congress Cataloging-in-Publication Data

Manthey, Cynthia M., 1961-
    Pre-K Math: concepts from global sources/by Cynthia M. Manthey
      p. cm.
    Includes bibliographical references and index.
    ISBN 0-89334-246-76 (hc). -- ISBN 0-89334-240-8 (pb)
    1. Mathematics -- Study and teaching (Preschool)   I. Title.
QA135.5.M354 1995
372.7'2--dc20

95-51841
CIP

ACKNOWLEDGMENTS

Sincere gratitude goes to the following list of wonderful people for enthusiastically sharing games from their own special childhood experiences. They have each helped to add beautiful aspects of diversity, global awareness, and multiculturalism to early childhood classrooms around the country. With utmost respect, I thank them for their gifts to children...the "peacemakers of tomorrow."

Elizabeth Lauersdorf
John Lauersdorf
Jeanine Lauersdorf
Pietro Pepitone
Rungrat Siriratanapanich
Renata Stier
Reverend Antonio Rodriguez
Ken Swift
Art Shegonee
Kamil Tanyeri
Serdar Atalay

TABLE OF CONTENTS

FOREWORD .... **IX**
A Note on Games from Around the World .... **x**
Primary and Secondary Theme Usage .... **xi**
Creatively Posting the Number of the Week .... **xii**
Items to Add to the Classroom .... **xiii**

ACTIVITITES FOR ALL UNITS **1**
   1   Making a Flannel Board 2
   2   Marble Numbers 4
   3   Number Mailbox 5
   4   Ms. Counter 6
   5   A Balance Scale 7
   6   A See-Saw Scale 8
   7   Counting in Various Languages 9
   8   Collections 11
       Letters to Parents 12

UNIT ONE: The Number 0 .... **13**
       Letter to Parents 14
   9   Cowrie - A Game from India 16
  10   Zero Bulletin Board 17
  11   Zero Art 18
  12   Zero Left 19
  13   Zero Snacks 20
  14   Two Yummy Carrots - A Fingerplay 21
  15   Little Birds in the Forest - A Subtraction Song 22
  16   Feeling Zero 23
  17   Zero Hero - A Puppet Show 24
  18   Zero Jar 26

UNIT TWO: The Number 1 .... **27**
  19   Jogo Anel - A Game from Brazil 28
  20   You're One of a Kind 29
  21   Show and Tell 30
       Letter to Parents 31
  22   What is One? 32
  23   Number One Necklace 33
  24   Number One Nature Walk 34
  25   Number One Nature Book 35
  26   The Sound of One 36
  27   One Autumn Leaf 37
  28   I Have One - A Fingerplay 38

UNIT THREE: The Number 2 .... **39**
   29   A Native American Guessing Game 40
   30   See Saw Game - A Game from Korea 41
   31   Twosday Tuesday 42
   32   Two Talk 43
   33   Sparkling Two's 43
   34   I Can Count So Many Ways - A Song or Poem 44
   35   Two-Two Train 45
   36   One-Two Marching 46
   37   Number Two Balance Beam 47
   38   Twobird Puppet 48
   39   Twobird - A Fingerplay 49
   40   Number Two Balancing Game 50

UNIT FOUR: The Number 3 .... **51**
   41   Cobra Cega - A Game from Brazil 52
   42   Dodgeball - A Version from the Congo 53
   43   Hop Little Frog 54
   44   Three Bee Puppet 55
   45   Three Bee - A Song or Poem 56
   46   Three Little Penguins - An Action Song or Poem 57
   47   Triangle Toss Game 58
   48   Magic Three Game 59
        Letter to Parents 60
   49   Clay Snowpeople 61
   50   Three Pink Flamingos - A Fingerplay and Song 62

UNIT FIVE: The Number 4 .... **63**
   51   Yut - A Game from Korea 64
   52   Mary's at the Kitchen Door - A European Nursery Rhyme 65
   53   I Left Four Lights On In My House - A Song or Poem 66
   54   Four Door 67
   55   Four Count Kazoo Parade 68
   56   How Many Make Four? - A Fingerplay 69
   57   Straw Drop 70
   58   Salt Numbers 71
   59   Number Four Garage 72
   60   Four Hunt 72
   61   4-legged Animal Prints 73
        Letter to Parents 74

UNIT SIX: The Number 5 .... **75**
   62   Istop - A Game from Turkey 76
   63   Peach Pits and Basket - A Native American Game 77

64	Pizza Toss	78
65	Silhouette Fives	79
66	Five Trees - A Fingerplay	80
67	Five Little Piggies - A Fingerplay	81
68	Five Fingers	82
69	Dive Five Puppet	83
70	Dive Five - A Puppet Poem	83
71	Five Ways to Get to the Store - A Fingerplay	84

UNIT SEVEN: The Number 6 .... **85**

72	Balloon - A Game from Thailand	86
73	Six Socks in Six Sacks - A Tongue Twister	87
74	Six Socks in Six Sacks Game	87
75	How Many is Six? - A Fingerplay	88
76	Pigtails	89
77	Six Sorting	90
78	6-legged Rock Insects	91
79	Six Mouse Puppet and House	92
80	Six Mouse Puppet Song	93
81	A Half-Dozen	94

UNIT EIGHT: The Number 7 .... **95**

82	Bottle Cap Soccer - A Game from the Congo	96
83	Hop Around the Days of the Week - A Game from Cuba	97
84	Number Seven Touch and Guess	98
85	Seven Globs of Trash - A Fingerplay and Song	99
86	Estimation Game	100
87	Book of Seven	101
88	Fishing for Sevens	102
89	Seven Snacks	102
90	Sevenocchio Puppet	103
91	Sevenocchio - A Puppet Show	104

UNIT NINE: The Number 8 .... **105**

92	Juego del Panuelo - A Game from Cuba	106
93	Eight Obstacle Course	107
94	Eight Circle Trace	108
95	Eight Little Balls Were Rolling - A Fingerplay and Song	109
96	Rolling Balls Subtraction	110
97	Number Eight Super Hero Masks	111
98	Eight O'Clock Bedtime - A Song	113
99	Number Eight Snacks	114

UNIT TEN: The Number 9 .... **115**

100	A Pallonate - A Game from Italy	116

101	Rock-n-Roll Nine Puppet	117
102	Rock-n-Roll Nine - A Puppet Song	118
103	Silver Nine	119
104	What's the Magic Number?	119
105	Hop Around a Nine	120
106	Recycle - A Song	121
107	Show Me Nine - A Clapping Rhythm Poem	122

UNIT ELEVEN: The Number 10 123

108	Gioco delle Figurini - A Game from Italy	124
109	Varanasi Numbers - A Game from India	124
110	Ten Prints	125
111	Baby Ben Puppet	126
112	Baby Ben - A Puppet Song	127
113	Ten Finger Prints Art	128
114	Number Ten Necklaces	129
115	Number Ten Cash Register	130
	Letter to Parents	131
116	Hip Wallets	132
117	I Can Count to Ten in French - A Song	133
118	Tour de Preschool	134

UNIT TWELVE: Backward Counting 135

119	Yakan Top - A game from Turkey	136
120	Rockets	137
121	Rockets, Blast Off! - A Movement Game	138
122	Ten Special Children Dolls	139
123	Ten Special Children - A Song or Poem	140
124	Thermometer	141
125	My Thermometer - A Song or Poem	142
126	Peacock Perception	143
127	A Measuring Turkey Baster	145
128	Numbers Incline Board	146
129	Tornado Tube	147
130	Hopping on a Caterpillar	148
131	Stairs	149

APPENDIX 151
ABOUT THE AUTHOR 154

FOREWORD

This book is filled with creative, tactile adventures which present basic whole math concepts to children ages of two to five years. Developmentally appropriate activities using art, bookmaking, and puppetry are your alternatives to boring worksheets. The whole math approach encourages young learners to visualize amounts as a whole. When a child first begins to take an interest in the quest to discover, "How many?" the initial approach is to count the items. The next step is to encourage a child to visualize and recognize amounts at a glance. For example, a three-year-old child who sees a plate of cookies may say, "There are one, two, three, four cookies." instead of saying, "I see four cookies." When a child is able to visualize amounts as whole numbers, the whole math approach can evolve. Later on, addition and subtraction become much easier to comprehend and compute. For example, it is much simpler to conclude that 5+2=7 by visualizing 5 and then adding 2 more (6, 7). The lengthy and more difficult method would be to count 1,2,3,4,5 and add 2 more (6, 7).

The whole math concepts within this book include:
- Numeral Identification
- Numeral Writing
- Differentiating Amounts
- Correlation of Numerals with Amounts
- Tactile Identification of Amounts
- Visualization of Whole Amounts
- Counting from Zero to Ten and from Ten to Zero
- Simple Addition
- Simple Subtraction
- Estimation

Math vocabulary and cognitive growth concepts include:
- Equal/Unequal
- More/Less
- Some/None/All
- Full/Empty
- Heavy/Light
- Shorter/Longer
- Shorter/Taller
- Smaller/Larger

A Note on Games from Around the World

Rules to children's games can vary greatly even within one city and, like other forms of folklore, are often changed. Likewise, it is often nearly impossible to determine the exact origins of games. Many of the games children play, such as "tag" or "hide and seek," can be found all over the world. People from many parts of the world proudly and happily shared these games to be passed on to others. Many mentioned that it was a sincere honor to share games from their native countries. With respect for these people, please always mention the names of the games in their proper languages, and speak of the countries from which they came. When you play a game subsequent times, ask the children to recall where the games are from to encourage their memory for this important information. To the wonderful people who shared these games, I am very grateful. They have each helped to promote multi-culturalism in preschool classrooms.

These cultural activities not only teach math concepts, but they also enrich integral social skills for the children. Furthermore, they can cause children to look at the world in a broader, more global sense – connecting them with children who, just like them, love to play but live far, far away. Please take into consideration the levels of emotional development within your group. Knowing that very young children have an extremely difficult time losing, you may easily adjust each one of these games to make them just as fun, and have "all winners."

It is strongly recommended that you use globes and atlases to locate the countries mentioned within the games. Encourage the children to ask questions so that together you may delve into many other interesting aspects of cultures from these countries. Ask your group of children and their families to share games from their own cultures. Children love to be creative and make up their own games, as well. They can become quite good at making up their own rules also, requiring them to use their emerging negotiation skills.

It is also important to let your children know that if a game is played in a particular country, it is certainly not the only game played in the country. Also, emphasize that not every child within the country plays that particular game. If you have a child in your group from a country which you are sharing a game from, ask that child if he or she has ever played it. If so, ask if the rules were the same.

Safety Note: Please refrain from allowing children under the age of four from playing games which use small pieces. Some games mentioned in this book require the use of items such as small shells, seeds, or pebbles which could pose as a potential choking hazard.

Primary and Secondary Theme Usage

This book serves well as a secondary unit book, intended to be used in conjunction with the primary unit book entitled *With Respect for Others: Activities for a Global Neighborhood.* The primary book contains unit topics on multiculturalism, safety, self-esteem, the five senses, and emotions. These are all broad spectrum topics based upon the philosophy of respect.

Secondary units, such as those included within this book, can be used to accompany your primary teaching unit or curriculum. Using primary and secondary units together provides a greater variety of activities which reinforce each topic. From a child's point of view, the inclusion of only one primary theme or topic can become tedious and overwhelming.

This book was intended for use in a manner similar to the following:

Sample Primary Unit		Secondary Unit
Week One	Self-Esteem and Saying "No"	The Number Zero
Week Two	African Cultural Aspects	The Number One
Week Three	Mexican Cultural Aspects	The Number Two
Week Four	The Sense of Sight	The Number Three
Week Five......		

The activities within this book focus on the development of environmental, self, and multicultural respect. Materials used within the activities are either free or inexpensive. Almost all of the activities are interchangeable and can be used in every number unit if the children enjoy them.

Please inform parents on a weekly basis as to what your primary and secondary units or basic curriculum will be. There are sample reproducible letters in units one and two for the children's parents, to start you on the path to utilizing parental involvement and at home learning.

Creatively Posting the Number of the Week

The following are some suggestions for posting your number of the week. Using a little effort and a lot of imagination, you can bring numbers to life for your children. The more senses you can stimulate, the better the children will learn the numbers.

Using different textures and colors when displaying numbers will stimulate the children's interest and encourage them to touch the numbers. Use yarn, colorful string, colored tape, drinking straws, pipe cleaners, twine, various types of sticks (including frozen pop sticks and tongue depressors), plastic six-pack rings, or bottle neck rings to shape your number of the week. Post it by attaching it to a wall or bulletin board with putty adhesive. Save all posted numbers in a file to be reused the next time you do numbers units.

Before your children arrive in the morning, you can write your number on an inflated balloon (do not tie it yet), and then let the air out. Tell the children that when the balloon is filled with air they will see what the magic number of the week will be. Blow air into the balloon and have the children watch as the number grows larger. The balloon can remain on display throughout the week for the children to see. You could also blow up the same number of balloons as your number of the week.

Write the number of the week backwards on the bottom of clear drinking glasses using a washable marker, so the children will see the number as they tip their glasses to take a drink.

Use a marker or paintbrush to write the number of the week on the children's napkins. Fold the napkins so that when they are unfolded, the number will become visible.

Make a large number on the floor using masking tape or colored tape. The children can then walk on it or use it as a balance beam. They will probably come up with other uses for it as well, such as a road for toy cars.

Vary the sizes of your posted numbers using huge ones as well as tiny ones. You may even make one that requires a magnifying glass to see.

Each week, as you post your number of the week, you can also post a piece of poster board with stickers corresponding to your number, i.e. during number 7 week, you may wish to display seven dinosaur stickers.

Place or hang the number of the week on the ceiling in several locations, including above the children's nap mats. When the children lie down, they will be surprised to see their special number of the week. Draw and cut this number from construction paper, and then post with putty adhesive.

Place the number of the week on walls and on the inside of the bathroom door so that the children will see the number when they shut the door.

Attach the number to your shirt or the children's shirts with colored tape, or construction paper fastened with masking tape. Pretend you have lost your number and attach it to your nose, your back, or the bottom of your foot. The children will enjoy many giggles as they locate your "missing" number for you.

Items to Add to the Classroom

The following is a list of items which will help you to promote math and number concepts for the children:

• Rulers and yard sticks for measuring, also encourage the use of unconventional items to measure with, such as shoes, crayons, bananas, etc.

• A small plastic wading pool without water works well as a sensory area. Add dry beans, raisins, uncooked macaroni, or other sensory items, measuring spoons and cups, and other cooking accessories. Allow the children to climb into the pool to play - even indoors.

• A scale for the children to weigh themselves and each other can be placed in a doctor's office dramatic play area with a note pad and pen for writing down weights.

• Tape measures, preferably not the metal kind, as used for measuring in sewing and carpentry.

• Calculators, battery-operated adding machines, or an abacus.

• Old telephones, rotary and touch tone. Check garage sales for these.

• Wind-up alarm clocks, stop watches, and egg timers.

• Spinners and dice from games.

• An inexpensive digital thermometer to be used under the arms only.

• Play money from a game or money you make easily yourself. Metal juice can lids and milk lids make terrific toy coins. Be sure to have enough coin purses or hip wallets for dramatic play.

Activities for All Units

These activities work well for all numbers, and are invaluable learning tools to incorporate in any early childhood education curriculum. While most of the games, songs, and learning activities in each unit can be adapted easily to fit other numbers, the first eight listed here are meant to be used continuously throughout the year.

ACTIVITY 1: Making a Flannel Board

Objectives: Counting, addition and subtraction, listening and memory skills, and dramatic play.

Materials:
- flannel
- various colors of felt
- a large piece of cardboard or an easel

Preparation: A flannel board can be a wonderful math manipulative. You can make a flannel board for your children at a nominal cost by purchasing flannel from a roll at a fabric or craft store. Hot glue or staple gun your flannel to a large, heavy piece of carboard. Felt squares are now available in a variety of skin-tone shades. When cutting out felt people for your flannel board, be certain to include diverse skin and hair colors. Fiskars brand scissors allow easy cutting for adults or children in making felt pieces for your flannel board. Cut out many (up to 20 or more) similar shapes, such as lions, fish, spaceships, teddy bears, or any other items your children are fascinated with at the moment. You can also cut out or buy numerals to correspond with amounts.

Procedure: Use the felt pieces to help the children learn counting, play guessing games, use simple addition and subtraction skills, or even understand concepts such as more/less and equal/unequal. The flannel board activities will progress through each unit, as the children become more competent with math concepts. To start, you may wish to tell stories to the children which involve different numbers of the felt shapes. For example, tell the story of *Goldilocks and the Three Bears*, using felt pieces in the shapes of a girl and three bears. Each time you say "three bears," point to the three bears on the board and ask, "How many bears are there?" This is just one way to ease the children into thinking about quantities and numbers.

Tips: Flannel boards are used in most classrooms as storytelling devices to capture young children's attention spans and involve them in the story. Please see the appendix for information on *The Flannel Board Storybook,* a complete resource book for constructing and using a flannel board effectively and improving storytelling skills.

Flannel Board Patterns

3

PRE-K MATH

ACTIVITY 2: Marble Numbers

Objectives: Numeral identification and writing, and motor skills.

Materials:
- eleven cardboard rectangles or styrofoam trays (styrofoam trays are available in the bakery or produce section of a supermarket)
- eleven marbles
- self-hardening clay or Homemade Play Dough (See Activity 50 for recipe)
- paints and brushes

Preparation: Place a ball of play dough on each styrofoam tray or piece of cardboard and press flat to about 1/4" to 1/2" thick. Using your index finger, lightly draw a number. Then press and roll a marble over the number to make an imprint. Allow the play dough to dry and paint the indented number. Acrylic paints work well for this.

Procedure: The children can place a marble on the number indentation on the clay. Holding the game, the child can manipulate the marble through the number without touching it. Less abled or less advanced children may wish to push the marble along with their finger. As the children become familiar with the numbers, you could also have them close their eyes and figure out which number they are feeling.

Tips: Never reuse styrofoam meat trays. They are porous and bacteria will remain despite attempts to sterilize.

PRE-K MATH   4

ACTIVITY 3: Number Mailbox

Objectives: Numeral identification, counting, and correlation of numerals with amounts.

Materials:
- a shoebox (no lid necessary)
- markers
- construction paper
- a metal paper fastener
- fifty-five used envelopes (if you know of a business office that has relocated recently, request their old business envelopes)
- red posterboard (5" by 2")
- scissors

Preparation: Turn the shoebox upside-down. Cut two of the corners along one of the narrow ends of the box to make a door that lifts open. Make a hole in the door for easier opening, or glue on a small bottle cap or spool as a knob. Write the numbers from zero to ten on the mailbox with a marker. Cut a mailbox flag from the red posterboard and attach the flag to the shoebox with a paper fastener. Draw and cut from construction paper the numbers from one to ten, making one 1, two 2's, three 3's, etc. Place each number in an envelope and label the outside of the envelope with the number. Group the envelopes together numerically with the two 2 envelopes together, the three 3 envelopes together, etc.

Procedure: In your number zero week, have a child check the mailbox to see how many letters (envelopes) are in it. The mailbox should be empty, and the answer will be, "Zero." When doing your number one week, again have the children take turns checking inside the mailbox at which time there will be one letter inside. Each child can open the envelope and find the number one.

Do the same with the envelopes in the mailbox at the beginning of each week until you reach number ten week, at which time there will be ten envelopes inside the mailbox each containing a number ten.

Tips: The mailbox can be used for many things other than math activities. You can put anything in a mailbox and it instantly becomes a mystery, children love to get presents and packages. In your storytelling, you can place objects from the story in the mailbox and have a child retrieve it when they are mentioned in the story. This involves the children in the story, and gets them focused on what you are saying.

ACTIVITY 4: Ms. Counter

Objectives: Counting, and visual and tactile identification of amounts.

Materials:
- paper cut from a large roll
- markers
- fabric scraps
- glue
- putty adhesive

Preparation: Using a large piece of roll paper and a marker, draw a child-size outline of a girl. Write her name, either a name the class decides on or "Ms. Counter," on the paper. Using putty adhesive, post Ms. Counter at the children's eye level. With each unit, attach different items to Ms. Counter with putty adhesive. The following are suggestions, some real, some easily made from construction paper:

Suggestions:
Unit One: One bat, one ball, one nose, one mouth, and one baseball cap.

Unit Two: Two ears, eyebrows, eyes, arms, legs, and feet. Please mention to the children that not everyone has two arms, hands, legs, or feet.

Unit Three: Three fish on a line, tools (a hammer, a saw, and pliers), different colored crayons, flowers, and pockets (use fabric squares).

Unit Four: Four birds, cherries, carrots, balloons, and paint brushes.

Unit Five: Five buttons for her shirt, fingers on each hand, toes on each foot, and keys.

Unit Six: Six leaves, shells, and pebbles.

Unit Seven: Seven ants, lady bugs, caterpillars, cocoons, and butterflies.

Unit Eight: A spider with eight legs, eight bees, snails, and dragonflies.

Unit Nine: Nine types of hats, such as a bike helmet, firefighter helmet, construction worker hat, police hat, baseball cap, winter stocking hat, football helmet, sombrero, top hat, and baker's hat.

Unit Ten: Stripes for pants (five for each leg), ten corn row braids, and ten rings for the fingers.

Tips: Making Ms. Counter's arms, legs, hands, toes, and fingers detachable gives you the opportunity to ask the children, "Does everyone have two arms, two legs, ten fingers and ten toes?" *Sports Illustrated for Kids* regularly features differently-abled athletes. Consider purchasing this issue and collaging the photos as part of a sports poster.

ACTIVITY 5: A Balance Scale

Objectives: Estimation, problem solving, understanding heavy, light, and equal.

Materials:
- a yard stick
- a hammer
- a nail
- two empty tissue boxes of the same size
- masking tape
- one piece of string 16" long, and four pieces 26" long

Preparation: Hammer a nail through the exact center of the yard stick and then remove the nail to expose the hole. Insert a piece of string and tie a knot at the end to attach it to the yard stick. Attach the remaining pieces of string to the holes of the tissue boxes as shown. Use masking tape to attach the strings which are connected to the tissue boxes to each end of the yard stick as shown.

Procedure: Hold up two objects and ask the children which one they think is heavier. Place each object into a tissue box on the balance scale and the heavier object will go down. After you show them how the heavier object moves it's side down farther, ask them again, "Now which object do you think is heavier?" Allow the children to experiment on their own with the scale. You may wish to challenge them to use several small objects to balance the scale. You can then introduce the concept of "equal" weights.

Tips: Attaching the balance scale directly under a counter, you can prevent the yard stick from moving into a vertical position when something heavy is placed on one side of it.

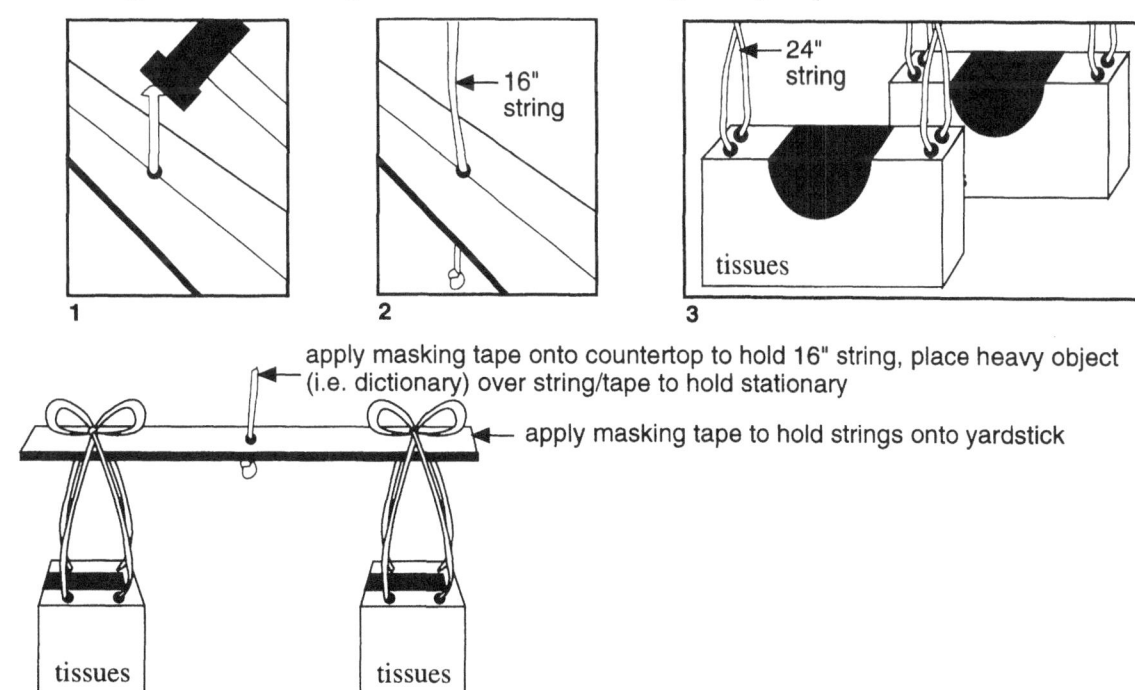

PRE-K MATH

ACTIVITY 6: A See-Saw Scale

Objectives: Counting, estimation, problem solving, understanding heavy, light, and equal.

Materials:
- a lightweight piece of wood such as particle board (suggested size: approximately 36"x5")
- wood block or narrow cardboard box
- foam pad or sponge

Procedure: Place the wood block or box on the floor or a small table. Place the sponge or pad on the box. Then, place the wood on the sponge to make a see-saw. Compare weights of many different objects. This may be used as a group and/or individual activity.

Tips: Not only can you compare the weights of two objects, but the see-saw scale works well for weighing different amounts of the same item. For example, place one apple on each side of the see-saw. Ask the children, "How many apples are on this side? How many are on the other side? Are they equal?" Add an apple to one side at a time, asking the children how many are on the scale and whether or not they are equal.

ACTIVITY 7: Counting in Various Languages

Objectives: Counting, familiarization with various foreign languages.

Note: Pronunciations are sometimes difficult to interpret, since there are tones used in some languages which are not found in others. If you know of someone who speaks or teaches these languages, consider inviting them to visit your class so that you and your children can hear the differences firsthand.

KISWAHILI: a language spoken in many parts of Africa
one: *moja* (MOjah)
two: *mbili* (mBEElee)
three: *tatu* (TAHtoo)
four: *nne* (Nnay)
five: *tano* (TAHno)
six: *sita* (SEEtah)
seven: *saba* (SAHbah)
eight: *nane* (NAHnay)
nine: *tisa* (TEEsah)
ten: *kumi* (KOO mee)

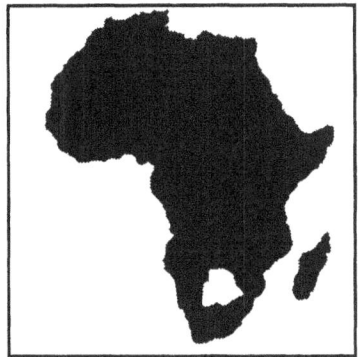

GERMAN
one: *eins* (ins) pronounced with a long "i"
two: *zwei* (svi)
three: *drei* (tri)
four: *vier* (FEEya)
five: *funf* (foonf)
six: *sechs* (secks)
seven: *sieben* (SEEben)
eight: *acht* (oct)
nine: *neun* (noyn)
ten: *zehn* (tsayn)

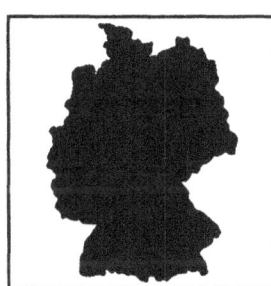

FRENCH
one: *un* (uhn) the "n" sound is made in the back of the tongue
two: *deux* (deuh)
three: *trois* (twah)
four: *quatre* (CATreh)
five: *cinq* (sank)
six: *six* (seese)
seven: *sept* (set)
eight: *huit* (weet)
nine: *neuf* (nuff)
ten: *dix* (deese)

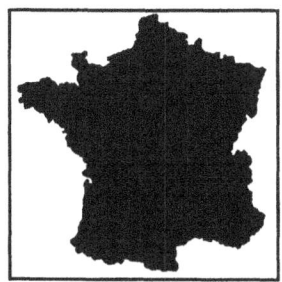

PRE-K MATH

SPANISH: a language spoken in Spain, Mexico, and most of South and Central America
one: *uno* (OOno)
two: *dos* (dose)
three: *tres* (trace)
four: *cuatro* (KWAHtro)
five: *cinco* (SINKoh)
six: *seis* (sayse)
seven: *siete* (SEEaytay)
eight: *ocho* (OHcho)
nine: *nueve* (NWAYvay)
ten: *diez* (dyesse)

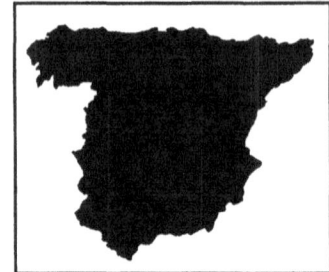

ITALIAN
one: *un* (oon)
two: *due* (DOOay)
three: *tre* (tray)
four: *quattro* (KWAHtro)
five: *cinque* (CHEENkway)
six: *sei* (SEHee)
seven: *sette* (SEHtay)
eight: *otto* (AWto)
nine: *nove* (NAWvay)
ten: *dieci* (DYEHchee)

ACTIVITY 8: Collections

Objectives: Sorting and counting skills, problem solving, and a sense of pride and individuality.

Materials:
- Letters to Parents

Preparation: Read carefully and reproduce the following parent notes for each child, sending each one home at the appropriate time. Please feel free to add your own ideas to these suggestions.

Suggestions:

Sorting: Have the children sort their collections by size, color, etc. Placing the items onto a large piece of white paper works well. If all of the objects are identical, have the children group the items into pairs or threes.

Counting: After the children count their items, help them write (or write for them) the number of items they have in their collections onto their white paper.

Subtraction: The children can each remove a certain number of items from their collections. Have them count the items. Replace the items which were removed. How many are there now?

Graphing: On a large piece of paper, write each child's name. Next to their names, use a marker to make dots to signify how many objects are in their collection (i.e. If Laurie has 23 pinecones, place 23 dots by her name while counting aloud with the children.) Then write the word "Total" under all of the names and make enough dots to correspond with the total number of collected items. Write down this number after counting aloud with the children once again. Post the graph for everyone to see.

Puzzle making: Have each child trace around each item in their collection (if possible) on a large piece of white paper. After removing the items, they can place them back in their original places like fitting pieces on a puzzle.

Memory game: Show the children each collection and have them guess whose it is. Or, you can go around the room as the children close their eyes and remove an item from several collections. When the children open their eyes, see who can guess which items are missing.

Individuality: Take each child's picture with his or her collection spread out on a large piece of white paper and display all of the pictures in a collage on the bulletin board. Take notes or tape record the children as they describe their collections and how they got them, why they like them, and why they chose to collect a particular item. If you take notes, send them home along with the photos of the children and their collections. Or, send each cassette recording home with each family.

LETTER TO PARENTS

Date:

Dear Parents:

We are beginning to learn early math concepts, such as numeral identification, counting, sorting, addition, and subtraction. Since it is easiest for young children to learn when they are using all of their senses, we need physical objects for each child to touch and see. Please begin a collection for your child. We will use these collections in many of our upcoming games and activities involving math skills. Some suggestions for collections are:

- buttons
- lids from various jars and bottles
- pencils
- shells
- rocks
- pinecones
- mismatched socks
- pennies

Please offer your child two or more suggestions from which he or she can make the final choice. Making choices helps children to feel important and capable. Find a special container, such as an empty tissue box, in which your child can keep the collected items.

Please do not send collections which include food or toys. Also, if your child often explores things orally, take care with which items you choose.

Please have your child bring his or her collection on _____.

Until that time, happy collecting!

Sincerely,

SECOND LETTER TO PARENTS

Date:

Dear Parents:

Just a reminder to please send your child's collection on _____.

Thank you for your important participation!

Sincerely,

UNIT ONE
The Number Zero

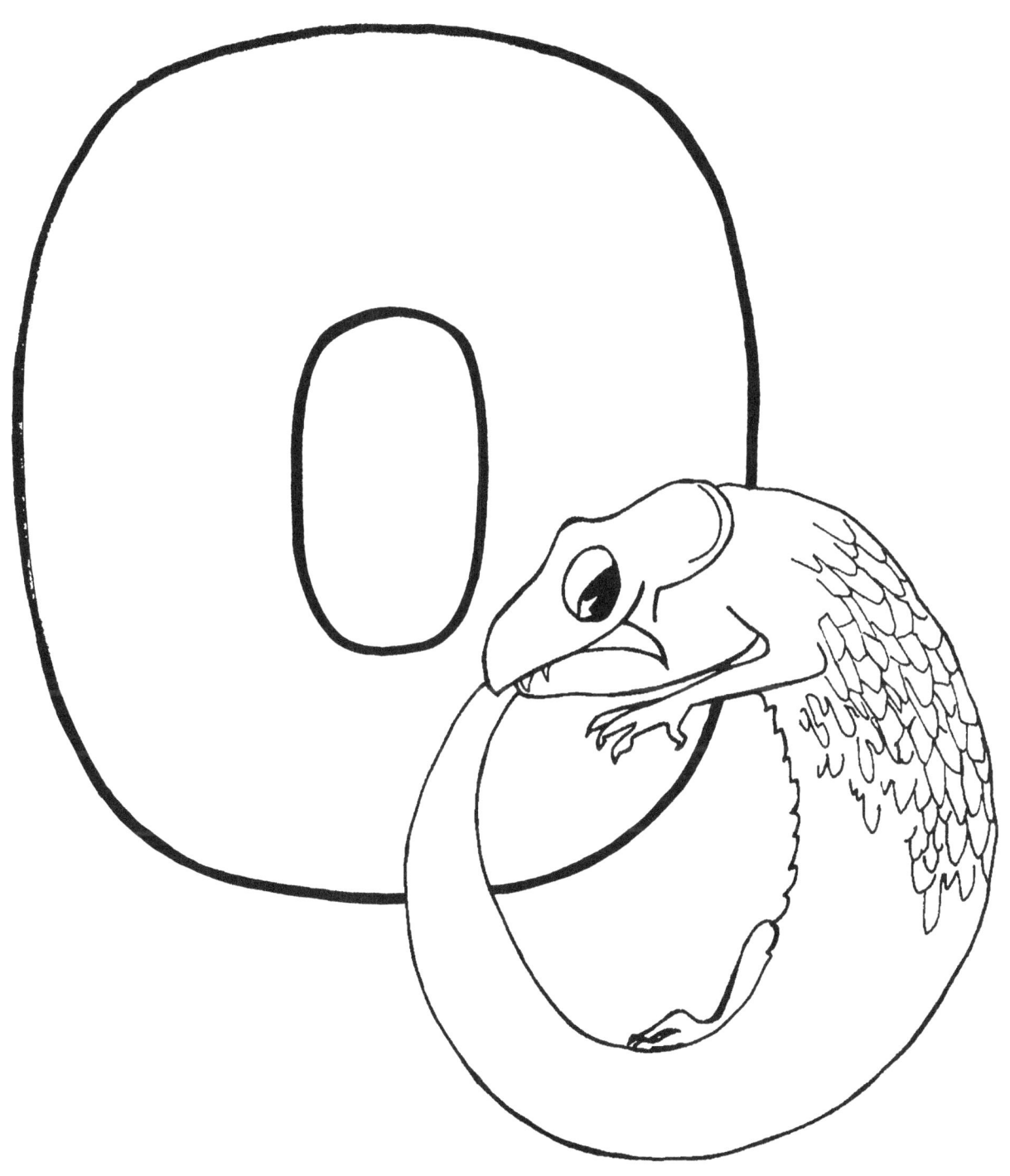

LETTER TO PARENTS

Dear Parents:

Date:

We are now beginning to learn early math concepts. This week our number will be "Zero." We will focus on a new number each week from zero to ten, and end with a week of counting backwards from ten to zero.

The concepts we will be exploring include:
- identification of numbers
- numeral writing
- differentiation of amounts
- tactile and visual identification of amounts
- correlation of numerals with amounts
- counting (forward and backward from ten to zero)
- simple addition
- simple subtraction
- estimation

The following are some easy ways to reinforce your child's learning of basic math concepts at home:

- Have your child count napkins, plates, and silverware as he or she helps set the table.

- While eating, occasionally ask your child, "How many crackers, beans, etc., do you have left on your plate?" Encourage simple counting whenever you can. This will also help occupy your child while in the car. Have them count red cars, trees, or anything that catches their interest.

- When you need to make a telephone call, have your child dial the number for you. Write the phone number of the daily local weather report or correct time message near the phone so that your child can make a phone call on his or her own.

- Have your child search for the number of the week and point it out while shopping. Look for numbers on signs, store products, cereal boxes, toys, license plates or page numbers in books.

A Note on Discarding Creations Made by Your Child: You may have come to the realization that everything your child creates and brings home cannot be saved without expanding the size of your home! When disposing of your child's art projects, please do it secretly or while your child is asleep to prevent tears and hurt feelings. Before disposing of art projects, please dissect them and return any reusable scraps. It's in the best interest of our environment. Thank you for your important involvement and your understanding.

Your Child's Natural Math Development

The ability to recognize and write numerals, and grasp basic math concepts is a natural, gradual process which develops within children at varying age levels. How early a child can recognize numbers or letters, count, or write numbers are not indicators of intelligence, nor are they results of good parenting or quality early childhood education. Parents often feel pressure to make sure that their children can recognize and write the entire alphabet and many, many numbers before kindergarten entrance. Not only is this unnecessary, but in most cases it's impossible. The following are some do's and don'ts to help you understand a child's emerging math skills. They will develop naturally with a little encouragement in the classroom and at home.

Do's
- Do allow writing to be play.
- Do realize the importance of not criticizing first attempts at writing.
- Do understand that the fine-motor development needed for writing develops later in many children. Much "scribbling" must happen first.
- Do give plenty of positive reinforcement. Smiles, encouragment, and kind words go a long way. For example, "You must be very proud of your work!" "You're putting lots of work into that, aren't you? Are you having fun?"
- Do offer high quality pencil grips for older preschool aged children who have difficulty holding pencils.
- Do keep blank sheets of paper, crayons, washable markers, pencils, pens, a calculator, used envelopes from your incoming mail, and child-safe scissors available for your child at all times. This will allow your child to make the choice to draw or write whenever he or she feels the desire. Using the small muscles for scribbling and coloring now will make number and letter-writing easier later.
- Do consider saving one item your child has written each month to place in a growth portfolio. It is exciting and encouraging for a child to see his or her own growth.

Don'ts
- Don't correct attempts at writing numbers, letters, or words since this may discourage a child from further writing attempts.
- Don't use lined paper. If you do use, do not expect your child to be able to write within the lines.
- Don't criticize if numbers are written incorrectly or backwards. This can be expected.
- Don't force writing practice, use of worksheets, flashcards or other rote methods that only place pressure on both you and your child.

Sincerely,

ACTIVITY 9: Cowrie - A Game from India

Objectives: Identification of an amount, small muscle hand-eye coordination, and multiculturalism.

Materials:
- small seeds or rounded shells (which will be called "cowries")
- chalk

Preparation: Locate a large playing surface, it should be flat and clear. Two to five players can play at one time. Use a stick or finger to make a small circle on the ground, or make one with chalk if playing on a sidewalk. Players stand at a designated location and attempt to pitch a cowrie into the circle.

Order of Play:
1. The player whose cowrie lands closest to the center of the circle starts first.
2. The person who tossed second starts first in the event of a tie.
3. The object of the game is to win the most cowries.

Procedure: Each player receives an equal number of cowries. The first player collects two or three cowries from the other players and drops them on the ground in the circle. The first player chooses two of the cowries on the ground and draws an imaginary line between them. The first player uses a finger flick to hit one cowrie towards the other. If the flicked cowrie hits the cowrie at which it was aimed, the player wins the cowrie which he or she hit and goes again. If more than one cowrie was hit, or if the cowrie was missed, it becomes the next player's turn. After all of the cowries have been won, a new collection of two or three cowries from each player starts a new game.

Tips: This game is often played by children in India with small cowrie shells or tamarind seeds. Some adults play it by placing a certain money value on each cowrie.

ACTIVITY 10: Zero Bulletin Board

Objectives: Identification of numeral, and correlation of numeral with an amount.

Materials:
- a bulletin board
- a number zero cut from construction paper

Procedure: Leave a bulletin board empty, and post a number zero next to it. When the children ask why it is empty, you can ask them, "How many items are on the bulletin board?" You can then help them with the answer (zero), reminding them that zero is your number of the week. Ask them if they can find the number zero that is near the bulletin board. If they answer, "None," tell them that there is a number that means "none." Encourage them to use the number zero rather than, "none" or "all gone."

ACTIVITY 11: Zero Art

Objectives: Numeral identification and writing.

Materials:
- paper
- crayons
- watercolor paints
- brushes

Procedure: Ask the children to use crayons to draw many zeros on their papers. Next, provide paints, water, and brushes and allow the children to make anything they wish. Before they begin to paint on their crayon zeros, ask them, "Do you think the paints will cover the zeros, or will we still be able to see the zeros after you have painted on them?"

Zero Patterns to Color

ACTIVITY 12: Zero Left

Objectives: Numeral and value identification, and correlation of numeral with an amount.

Materials:
- snack items (such as crackers)
- napkins
- a crayon or marker

Preparation: Write or draw a small number zero on the back of each child's napkin.

Procedure: Give each child a small portion of crackers. When they have eaten all of their crackers, ask the children how many crackers they have left. (Zero) Tell the children they can turn over their napkins to see how many crackers are left. Please do not insist that the children eat all of their crackers if they do not wish to. In this case, you may wish to take the leftover crackers and place them into a plastic bag to crumble and feed to birds. After the child puts them into a bag, ask, "Now how many are on your napkin?"

PRE-K MATH

ACTIVITY 13: Zero Snacks

Objectives: Numeral identification.

Procedure: Serve bagels as a snack and tell the children they each get to "Eat a number zero," since bagels are shaped like the number zero. Ask the children what else they eat that is shaped like a zero. You can bring in several examples of these, including doughnuts, certain cereals, lifesavers candies, etc.

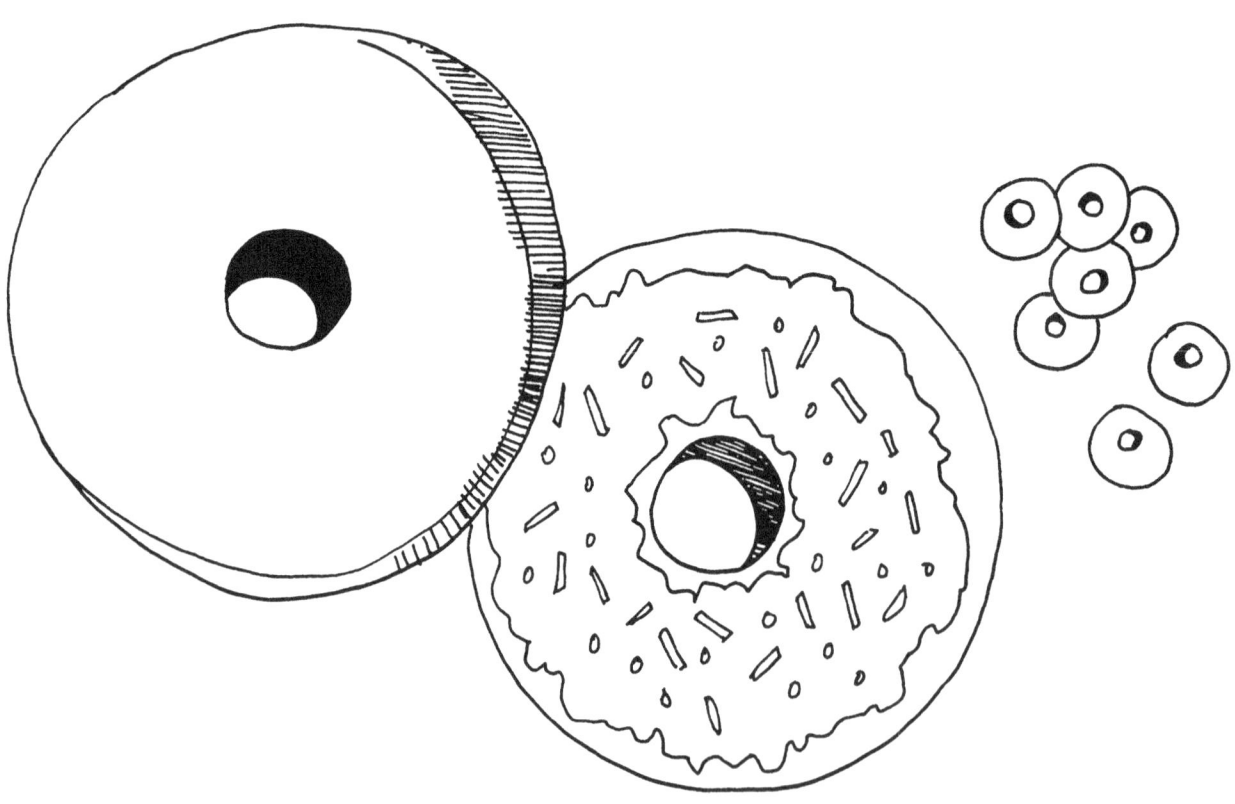

ACTIVITY 14: Two Yummy Carrots - A Fingerplay

Objectives: Identification of an amount, subtraction, listening and motor skills.

Two Yummy Carrots
(A Riddle)

Two yummy carrots, sitting on a plate.
I said, "Mommy, these carrots look great!"
I ate those carrots like such a hero.
And now on my plate - there are ____.
(Answer: Zero)

ACTIVITY 15: Little Birds in the Forest - A Subtraction Song

Objectives: Addition, subtraction and respect for the forest as a home for animals.

Procedure: One child walks to the center of the room with arms flapping, and another child joins in as each new verse is sung. When subtracting, the children will leave the circle flying away one by one with each new verse.

Little Birds in the Forest

There was one little bird in the forest-
and he sang a happy song.
There was one little bird in the forest-
and he said, "Won't you please come along?"

There were two little birds in the forest-
and they sang a happy song.
There were two little birds in the forest-
and they said, "Won't you please come along?"

Continue to add another child until all of the children are in the circle. Then the first child that entered the circle will be the first to leave as you sing:

There were ___ little birds in the forest.
They were so happy and gay.
There were ___ little birds in the forest.
And then one of the birds flew away.

Continue to subtract by having the children "fly away" from the circle one by one until all of the children have "flown away."

ACTIVITY 16: Feeling Zero

Objectives: Tactile numeral identification.

Materials:
- pipe cleaners
- scissors
- tape
- a small paper or fabric bag

Preparation: Cut pipe cleaners and bend them to make several different numbers between zero and ten. Wrap the sharp ends of the pipe cleaners with tape.

Procedure: Have the children take turns placing a hand inside the bag to feel and identify the number zero. When they have found the zero, they can remove it from the bag. Challenge more advanced children by using more numbers. You know best what your children's developmental levels are.

ACTIVITY 17: Zero Hero - A Puppet Show

Objectives: Identification of numeral and an amount, subtraction, and dramatic play.

Materials:
- an almost empty box of crackers
- an almost empty cereal box
- an egg carton with one egg
- an empty milk carton
- a puppet with a zero on its chest and a super hero cape

Preparation: Construct a puppet from an old sock or paper bag, or use the illustration provided and attach to a tongue depressor or popsicle stick. (Please consider having this be a female puppet other than white, Euro-American, since white males have consistently dominated the superhero market for so long.)

Puppet Show: Have the puppet fly into the room announcing that he or she is the Zero Hero. Have the puppet tell the children that he or she can make things become zero. Then the Zero Hero can go to the diffferent food items and pretend to eat each one (at which time you will pour the food into a grocery bag). Each time the puppet eats some food, ask the children, "How many are left?" Then the puppet can sing or chant, "I'm Zero Hero! I love to make zero!" Invite the children to join in.

Small Puppet Pattern

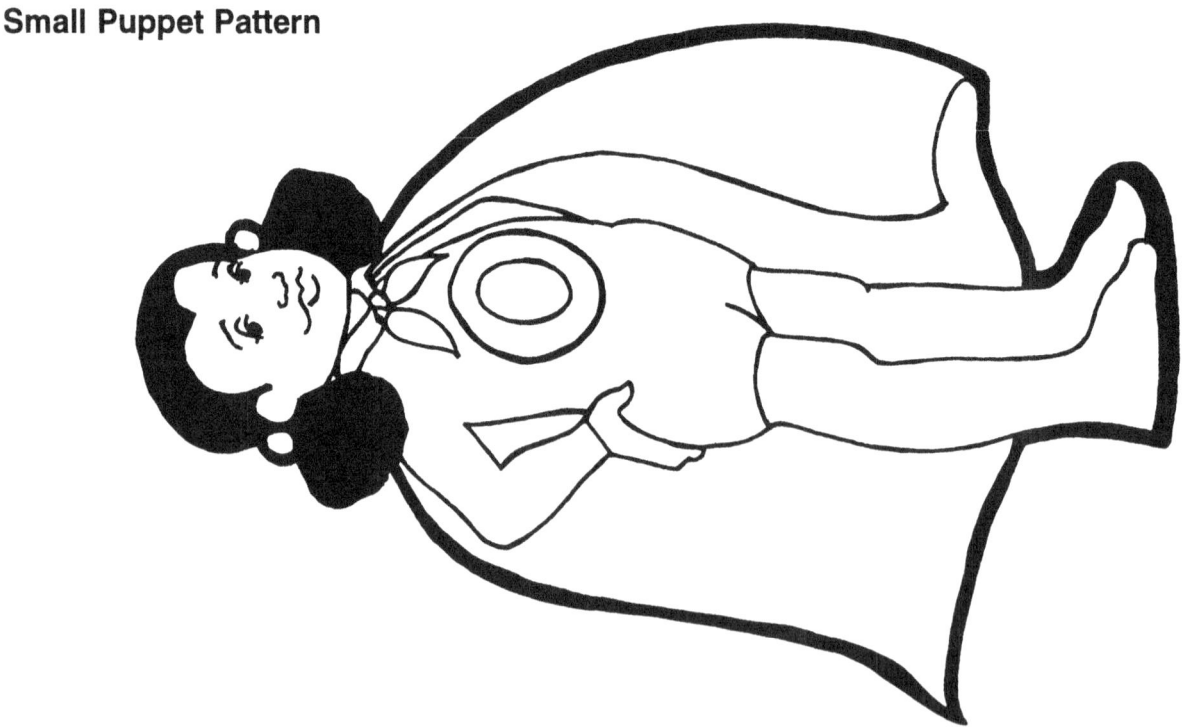

Big Puppet Pattern

ACTIVITY 18: Zero Jar

Objectives: Identifying and differentiating amounts, full/empty, heavy/light, and estimation.

Materials:
- three clean, clear, empty plastic containers (such as peanut butter jars)
- many small items (marbles, jelly beans, buttons, etc.) to fill one of the jars

Preparation: Leave the first jar empty. Place one of the small items into the second jar. Fill the third jar with marbles or beans, etc.

Procedure: Show the children the jars. Ask them how many items are in the jar containing one item. Then ask them how many are in the empty jar. Tell the children that since there is nothing in the jar, there are zero items in it. Show them the full jar. Ask them to guess how many items are in it, telling them that this kind of guessing is called "estimation."

Ask the Children: Which jar is full, and which is empty? Which one would be heavier? Which jar has the most items/the least items?

Tips: Attach a paper zero to the empty jar. Leave the jars out all week for the children to see, hold and explore.

UNIT TWO
The Number One

ACTIVITY 19: Jogo Anel (JOgo ahNEHL) - A Game from Brazil

Objectives: Visual and tactile identification of an amount, small muscle and hand-eye coordination, and multiculturalism.

Materials:
- one inexpensive ring, either metal or plastic

Procedure: The children stand in a circle holding their hands together in front of them. The child who is "it" holds a ring in his or her hands and stands in the center of the circle. Then the child who is "it" walks around to each child and secretly passes the ring to one of the other children. Then one child is allowed one guess which child is now holding the ring. If that child is right, then he or she gets to stand in the center (and be "it") and secretly pass the ring to someone. If that child guesses incorrectly, then the child who is holding the ring becomes "it."

ACTIVITY 20: You're One of A Kind!

Objectives: Identification of numeral and an amount; correlation of numeral with an amount.

Materials:
- award patterns
- empty cereal boxes or cardboard
- scissors
- permanent marker
- masking tape
- glue
- tin foil or shiny scrap paper (such as a deflated mylar balloon, a potato chip bag with a shiny interior, or shiny candy wrappers, which have been washed and dried)

Preparation: Cut the shiny scraps and glue them onto the awards cut from the cereal boxes. Using a permanent marker, write each child's name above and the phrase, "is 1 of a kind" below.

Make one of these awards for each child, and allow the marker and glue to dry. Place a loop of masking tape on the back of each award and give one to each child, reminding them how unique and special they are. There is only one of them in the whole world!

Ask the Children: How many "you's" are there in this class? How many in the world? No one else in the world is just like you, do you you know how special that makes you?

29 PRE-K MATH

ACTIVITY 21: Show and Tell

Objectives: Counting, addition, subtraction, and identification of an amount.

Materials:
- one of any item from home. (See the following reproducible parent letter)

Procedure: Have the children sit on the floor in a circle with the items they brought from home in front of them. Ask the children how many items they have in front of them. (One) Then have the children place the items behind them. Ask them how many are in front of them now. (The answer should be "Zero," rather than "None" or "All gone.")

Next, have the children place their items in the center of the circle. Count the number of children. Tell them how many children there are. Then ask, "How many items are in the middle of the circle?" First have the children guess how many they think there are, and then allow the children to count the items. Is the number the same as the number of children?

Ask the Children: Do you have a story about your item that you'd like to share?

Tips: While the items are in the center of the circle, you might like to play memory games or sorting games with the children. For example, after everyone has showed their item, point to an item in the circle and see if the children can remember who brought it. You could also point out similarities and differences in the items, or sort the items. "How many stuffed animals are in the circle?"

LETTER TO PARENTS

Date:

Dear Parents:

Please send one item with your child tomorrow which we will use for our math activities. The item can be a button, a jar lid or just about anything, but the children will be more involved in our activities if you send along something which interests them. Please DO NOT send food items or toys which can be broken. If you send along a toy, make sure that it can be identified as belonging to your child. For example, a piece of masking tape with your child's name on it can be placed on a flat surface.

Thank you for your valuable participation, bringing something from home makes the activities that we do together extra special and memorable.

Sincerely,

ACTIVITY 22: What is One?

Objectives: Identification of numeral and an amount, correlation of a numeral with an amount, fine motor skills, and fostering a love of books.

Materials for each child:
- five 3" x 5" unlined index cards
- scissors
- crayons or markers
- glue (school glue isn't strong enough)
- a photocopy of each child's photograph
- four different stickers
- a stapler just for the teacher

Preparation: Place the photos of the children side by side face down in a copy machine. Make photocopies so that you have a copy of each child's photograph. Cut out each one to separate them.

Procedure: The children may place a sticker of their choice onto each page (index card), and glue the copy of their photo onto a separate page as well. Show the children how to draw a number one, a straight line. If they wish, they can draw a number one on each page to indicate how many items there are on each page. After the pages are dry, staple each child's book together, making the photo page the last (and most special) one.

Sample 3" x 5" card with space for child's name

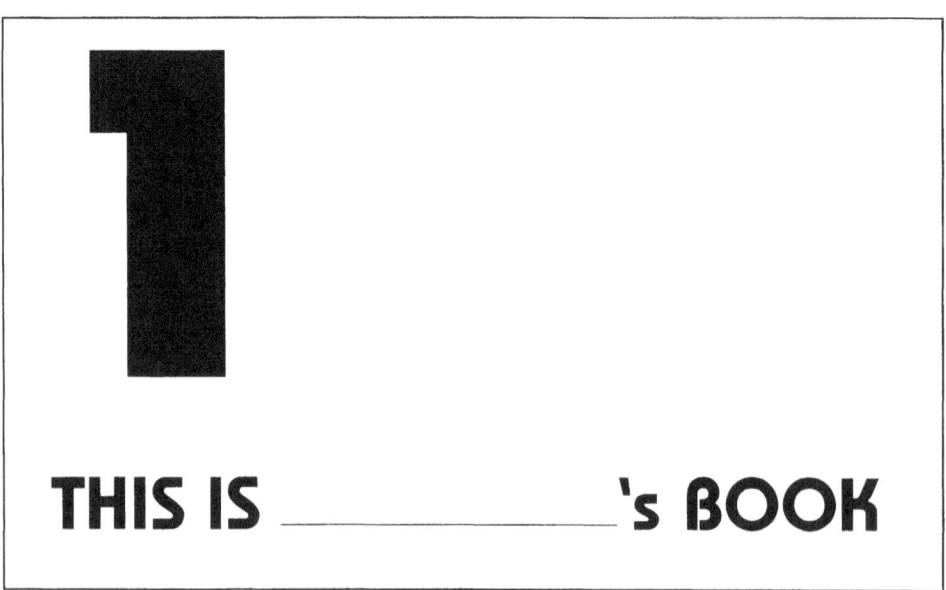

ACTIVITY 23: Number One Necklace

Objectives: Visual and tactile identification of an amount, and correlation of numeral with an amount.

Materials for each child:
- transparent tape
- a 24" piece of yarn
- an empty thread spool (OR have the children each make their own large bead out of Homemade Play Dough)
- non-toxic acrylic paints
- brushes

Preparation: Wrap one end of each of the pieces of yarn in tape for easy threading. Give each child paints and brushes and spools or beads. To make beads, have the children make any shape with Homemade Play Dough and poke a hole through it with a cocktail straw. Allow plenty of time to dry before painting.

Procedure: Have the children use the paint to decorate their spools or beads. After the paint is dry, allow the children to insert the tape-wrapped end of their yarn through their spool. Tie together the ends of each child's piece of yarn to complete their necklaces which contain one very special item.

Tips: You can check the yellow pages in your phone book for "Tailors" or "Alterations" and request that they save empty thread spools for you. See Activity 50 for a recipe for Homemade Play Dough.

ACTIVITY 24: Number One Nature Walk

Objectives: Tactile and visual numeral identification, and observational skills.

Procedure: Take a walk through a field or forest with the children. Have them each search for one item that resembles the number one (no living plants please) such as a twig, a wide blade of grass, the stem from a weed, a narrow rock, a seed from a tree, or a pine needle. Have the children carry their one-shaped items back to the classroom.

Tips: If the children have trouble finding one-shaped items, or a wide variety of one-shaped items, have them look for zero-shaped items, as well. Tell them that any round items will do. You may wish to collect leaves on this nature walk, as well, to gather materials for Activity 28: One Autumn Leaf.

ACTIVITY 25: Number One Nature Book

Objectives: Visual and tactile identification of an amount, visual identification of numeral, correlation of numeral with amount, fine motor skills, and fostering a love of books.

Materials:
- nature items which the children collected in preceding activity
- a half sheet of construction paper for each child
- glue
- a hole punch
- yarn

Procedure: Have each child glue their item vertically to resemble a number one onto his or her piece of construction paper. Have the children write their names on their papers, or write their names for them. Hole punch and bind the pages together with yarn to make one large book. Allow the children plenty of time to take turns looking through the book.

Tips: If any of the children does not want to give up his or her item as a page in the cooperative book, please do not force them to participate. Sometimes children form emotional attachments with items which they've collected, or want to keep their treasures for other reasons. After the book is complete, ask to display the book in your library, or leave the book out in the room for the children to play with.

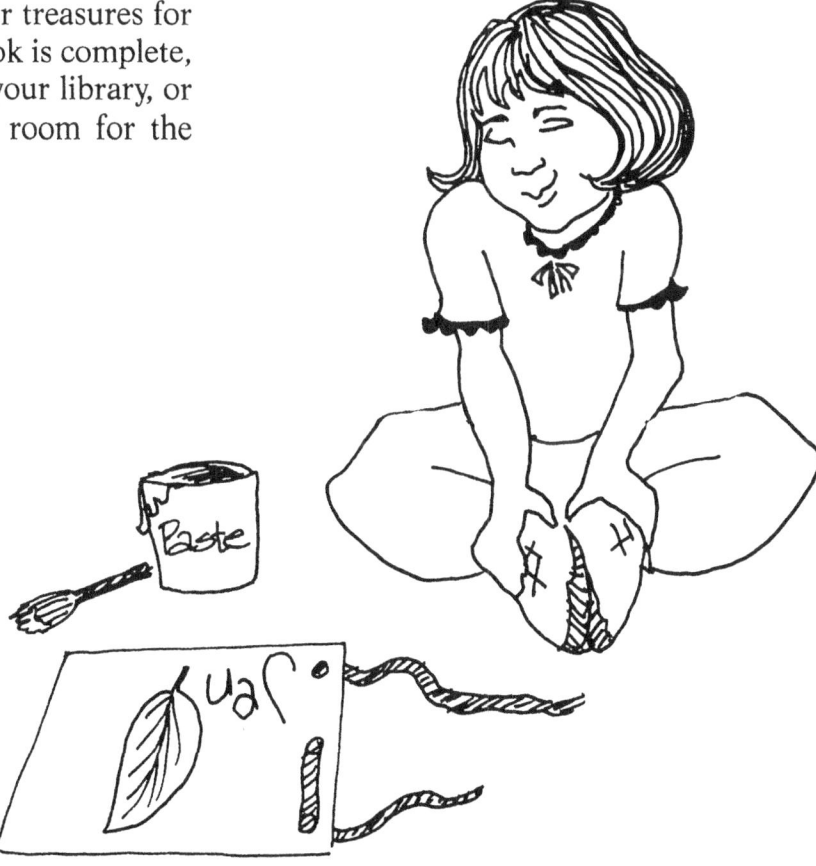

ACTIVITY 26: The Sound of One

Objectives: Auditory and visual identification of an amount, listening skills, tactile skills, and estimation.

Materials:
- an empty coffee can
- plastic milk lids

Procedure: Shake the empty coffee can and ask the children how many lids are in the can. (Zero) Show them the inside of the empty can. Turn your back to the children and place one milk lid in the can and shake it again. Ask the children how many milk lids are in the can now. Then turn your back again and place several milk lids in the can and shake it. Have the children estimate how many are in the can. Let them take a quick peek and guess again. Write down their estimated numbers and count the lids to find out how close they came with their estimations.

Ask the Children: If you could not hear, how could you figure out how many lids were in the can? When you shake the can, can you feel vibrations? If you could not see, how could you know how many lids were in the can?

Tips: You can also conduct this activity by having the children reach into the can to feel how many lids there are.

PRE-K MATH 36

ACTIVITY 27: One Autumn Leaf

Objectives: Identification of amount.

Materials:
- one colorful leaf for each child (please allow children to choose their own leaves)
- a hole punch
- yarn
- scissors
- small pieces of construction paper
- glue poured into plastic caps or lids
- paint brushes

Preparation: Have each child collect a colorful or interesting leaf.

Procedure: Have each child brush both sides of his or her leaf with a thin layer of glue and place the leaf onto a small piece of construction paper. Allow these to dry. Punch a hole at the top of each paper, insert a long piece of yarn and tie the ends together. The leaves will retain their beautiful colors, and can be used as ornaments or necklaces. These make nice fall gifts for parents.

ACTIVITY 28: I Have One - A Fingerplay

Objectives: Identification of an amount, listening skills, and motor skills.

I Have One

I have one nose - and it goes sniff, sniff, sniff, achoo!
(point to nose)

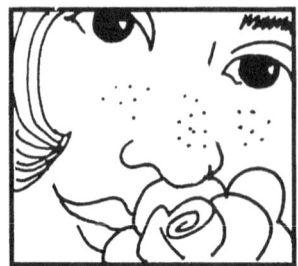

I have one mouth - and it goes talk, talk, talk, munch, munch.
(make hands do talking motions)

I have one neck - and it goes this a-way, that a-way,
(turn head left, then right)

this a-way, that a-way.
(look up and then down)

I have one belly button - it's so funny! It just sits there in the middle of my tummy!
(point to belly button)

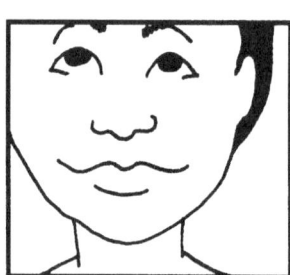

And my tummy goes tickle, tickle, tickle! *(tummy tickles optional.)*

UNIT THREE
The Number Two

ACTIVITY 29: A Native American Guessing Game

Objectives: Counting, addition, small muscle coordination, and multiculturalism.

Materials:
- eight wooden dowels, 12" x 1/8"
- a black marker (to be used by the teacher only)
- a folded blanket
- twenty toothpicks (ten of one color and ten of another)

Preparation: Use the marker to color 7 of the dowels as shown in the illustration. Color the remaining dowel only in the center.

Procedure: Divide the children into two teams. Place a folded blanket on the floor between the two teams, who are seated facing each other. Have two children on one team place the sticks under the blanket. Both children then can reach under and pick up a four sticks each, grasping them at the ends. Their hands should cover the black marks at the ends of the sticks. A member of the opposing team then guesses which bundle the differently marked stick is in. If the guess is correct, then it becomes their turn to hold the sticks. If the guess is incorrect, the team holding the sticks scores a point (receiving a toothpick as a point marker) and has another turn to hold the sticks. Determine a certain toothpick color for each team. You may wish to give each team a container to hold their toothpicks in. The first team to receive ten toothpicks wins the game.

Tips: If this game is too complicated for your age group, you might want to hold the sticks, yourself, and simply allow the two teams of children to guess. The Native American Nation from which this game originated is not known. There are a great number of guessing games and a number of variations as to how this particular game is played. One version involves singing and drumming while playing. Originally, real sticks with their bark removed were used by Native Americans playing this game. Instead of using a marker to darken certain areas of the sticks, the sticks were once actually carved (with notches or indentations) in the areas between what are now black marks. Where toothpicks are now used to keep score, stiff prairie grasses or small sticks were once used.

Marks on sticks (dowels) to be made as follows:

7 dowels have marks like this:

8th dowel has marks like this:

ACTIVITY 30: See-Saw Game - A Game from Korea

Objectives: Counting, subtraction, addition, visual estimation of distance, visualization of an amount, small muscle and hand-eye coordination.

Materials:
- a 12" wooden ruler
- a small 2" x 2" piece of polyfoam sponge
- two 4" x 3" polyfoam sponge pieces
- a small bowl or basket

Preparation: Cut the two 4" x 3" pieces into shapes resembling children. Place the 2" x 2" piece of sponge under the ruler on a table top.

Procedure: The children can use the ruler as a see-saw toy. They can catapault the child-shaped sponges into the air and attempt to catch them in the basket. Use the sponges to show the children how the game is really played, (see below) but explain to them that because of safety reasons, they will play the game only with the sponge dolls.

The Original Game: A long board is placed on the ground. A folded mat or blanket is placed under the center of the board. Two children play. One stands on one end of the board. The other child jumps onto the board, sending the first one up into the air. Then, that child lands on the board, sending the other child up into the air, and so it continues. With a lot of practice, the children can become quite skilled at this and go very high into the air.

Tips: Due to possible injury, do not play this version of the original game with the children. A child friend of mine told me of this game which she played when she was a preschooler and living in Korea. She thought this game would be too dangerous for young children to play, but still wanted them to know about it.

ACTIVITY 31: Twosday Tuesday

Objectives: Identification of numeral and an amount.

Procedure: Post a large sign that says, "2's Day, Tuesday." Explain to the children that every week there is a Tuesday, and on this particular Tuesday you will be celebrating the number two. The Show and Tell Game in the preceding unit can be played using the children's shoes. You can use this opportunity to have a party of two's: two snacks, two songs, two rhymes, two minutes of dancing, two storytimes, two naps, etc.

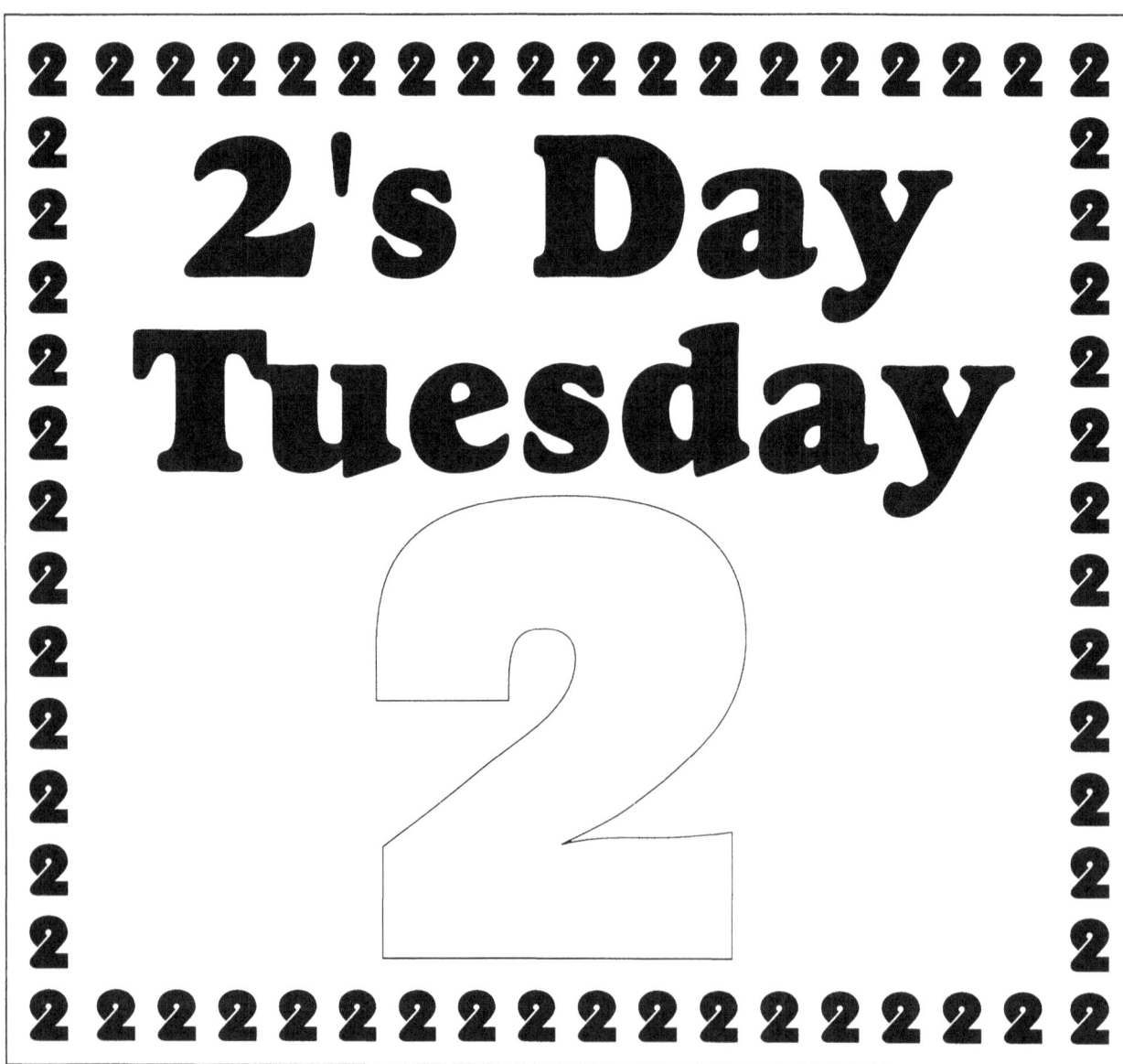

ACTIVITY 32: Two Talk

Objectives: Auditory and rhythmic identification of an amount.

Procedure: Say say everything everything twice twice during during certain certain parts parts of of the the day day. Speak slowly so the children will understand you. Ask them how many times you are saying each word. Soon they will be speaking your new language with you.

Tips: You could vary this activity by whispering or singing the repeated word. Or, practice having the children repeat what you say. The funnier the lines you give the children to repeat, the more they'll pay attention. For example, try having the children finish repeating lines from Dr. Seuss or a favorite storybook. You can also divide the class into two sections and sing lines of songs twice, seeing who can sing the loudest.

ACTIVITY 33: Sparkling Two's

Objectives: Numeral writing and identification, fine motor skills, and artistic expression.

Materials for each child:
- a paper towel
- a small amount of glitter in a plastic lid or other container
- thick yarn
- a marker for the teacher

Preparation: Write a number two with a marker on each paper towel. Place a piece of yarn on one of the number two's to determine length. Then, cut a piece for each child to use. Older or more advanced children can do this preparation themselves.

Procedure: Have the children dip their pieces of yarn into the glue. Next, have them lay the yarn on the number two on their paper towel. They can then sprinkle glitter over their two's. Allow the two's to dry. After the children have made their sparkling two's, allow them to create masterpieces of their own with the remaining materials.

PRE-K MATH

ACTIVITY 34: I Can Count So Many Ways - A Song or Poem

Objectives: Counting, counting in pairs to ten, in both Spanish and English.

I Can Count So Many Ways

Chorus: I can count so many ways.
            I'm proud of the way I can count.
            (repeat)

Verses: I can count by one's to ten.
            I can count by one's to ten.
            1 – 2 – 3 – 4 – 5
            6 – 7 – 8 – 9 – 10. *(Chorus)*

            I can count by two's to ten.
            I can count by two's to ten.
            2 – 4 – 6 – 8 – 10.
            Let's do it once again.
            2 – 4 – 6 – 8 – 10.
            I can count by two's to ten. *(Chorus)*

            I can count in Spanish to ten.
            I can count in Spanish to ten.
            Uno, dos, tres –
            cuatro, cinco, sies –
            siete – ocho – nueve – diez. *(Chorus)*

            I can count backward from ten.
            I can count backward from ten.
            10 – 9 – 8 – 7 – 6 –
            5 – 4 – 3 – 2 – 1. *(Chorus)*

Tips: See Activity 7 for the pronunciations of the Spanish numbers in this song.

ACTIVITY 35: Two-Two Train

Objectives: Identification of numeral and an amount, correlation of numeral with an amount, and fine motor skills.

Materials:
- construction paper
- scissors
- yarn
- different types of animal stickers (two of each per child)
- transparent tape in a dispenser

Preparation: Draw and cut out several number two's in large, blocked form for each child. Children who wish to help you cut out two's may assist. Cut several at once to save time.

Procedure: Have the children place their animal stickers on their number two's. The children may now use tape and yarn to connect the two's together and make a train. Either post the train up in the classroom, or leave it out as a pull toy for the children to play with.

ACTIVITY 36: One-Two Marching

Objectives: Counting, gross motor skills, and rhythmic and auditory identification of an amount.

Materials:
- two thick wooden dowels for each child

Preparation: Line up the children in groups of two. If there is an odd amount of children, you can be someone's partner. Count the children by two's as they line up, and tell them that they are going to be in a parade.

Procedure: Give each child two wooden dowels to tap together, and begin marching as you count, "One-two, one-two." If there are children who choose to watch rather than participate, please respect their wishes.

Tips: If dowels are not available, the children can clap their hands. If using dowels, however, be sure to warn the children not to hit them too hard, it's possible for them to break and splinter.

ACTIVITY 37: Number Two Balance Beam

Objectives: Numeral identification, gross motor skills, and early writing skills.

A) Outdoor Version Materials:
- sidewalk chalk for warm weather
- a spray bottle filled with water and food coloring for snowy weather

Preparation: Draw a very large (approximately twelve feet long) number two with sidewalk chalk, or make it in the snow with your footprints. Spray the number two-shaped tracks in the snow with the colored water.

B) Indoor Version Materials:
- a large piece of paper from a roll
- putty adhesive or two-sided tape
- markers
- scissors

Preparation: Draw a number two on a large piece of paper, cut it out, and secure it to the floor with putty adhesive or two-sided tape.

Procedure: The children can walk or drive toy cars on the number two. Have them try not to step off the two while practicing different walks. Have them trot, or skip, or walk backwards along the two.

PRE-K MATH

ACTIVITY 38: Twobird Puppet

Objectives: Numeral identification.

Materials:
- either blue pipe cleaners or blue construction paper
- yellow or orange construction paper
- blue feathers (from school supply catalog or craft supply store)
- scissors
- glue
- a marker

Preparation: Make a number two shape from either a pipecleaner or piece of construction paper. Use a marker to draw eyes on your paper number two, or if using pipecleaner, glue on sequin or construction paper eyes. Glue on wings (feathers) and a construction paper beak.

Procedure: Use this puppet to introduce any of your "Two Activities" and in the fingerplay in Activity 40.

ACTIVITY 39: Twobird - A Fingerplay

Objectives: Identification of numeral and an amount, counting, listening and motor skills.

Twobird

Twobird, Twobird is a little bluebird.
Twobird, Twobird sings two tweets – "Tweet, tweet."

Twobird, Twobird is a little bluebird.
Twobird, Twobird has two eyes – "Blink, Blink."

Twobird, Twobird is a little bluebird.
Twobird, Twobird has two wings – "Flap, Flap."

Twobird, Twobird flies all day.
He sings two tweets and flies away.

Fly, fly - tweet, tweet.
Bye, bye - tweet, tweet.
Fly, fly - tweet, tweet.
Bye, bye - tweet, tweet.

PRE-K MATH

ACTIVITY 40: Number Two Balancing Game

Objectives: Identification of numeral and an amount.

Materials:
- a box with a large number two drawn on it
- a pair of similar small objects for each child (2 erasers, 2 blocks, 2 rocks, etc.)

Preparation: Have each child stand on one side of the room with the number two box directly across from them. As they hold their hands in front of them (palms down), place the two objects on the backs of their hands.

Procedure: The object of this activity is to make it to the two box without dropping your objects. When they reach the box, they should drop thier objects in one at a time saying, "One, two!"

Tips: For beginners, try balancing the toys with the palms facing upward.

UNIT FOUR
The Number Three

ACTIVITY 41: Cobra Cega (CObrah SEHgah) - A Game from Brazil

Objectives: Counting, addition, sensory awareness, and listening skills.

Materials:
- a blindfold
- a large, safe area free from obstacles or stairs

Procedure: The blindfolded child is "it" and moves around the room attempting to find the other children and tag them. When a child is tagged, he or she becomes "it." Tell the child who is "it" that he or she must use listening skills to locate the others.

Tips: To expand upon math concepts, you can keep a tally of how many children were tagged, how many children were playing, and how many times each child was tagged. These concepts make interesting graphs. Translated, this game is called "The Blind Snake Game." You may use this opportunity to discuss blindness with the children, and how other senses compensate for the loss of one.

ACTIVITY 42: Dodgeball: A Version from the Congo

Objectives: Math concepts of more/less, empty/full, subtraction, counting, and gross motor skills.

Materials:
- a soft ball (one made from fabric scraps tied together works well)
- transparent, unbreakable bottles with narrow necks (one less than the number of children playing)
- a sand surface or gym mats

Preparation: Draw a large circle in the sand with a stick, or designate boundaries with objects such as shoes. The diameter of this circle will depend upon how far the children can throw. Place the empty bottles in the very center of the circle, where they must remain throughout the game.

Procedure: One player is "it" and must remain outside the circle while throwing the ball at the other players. The other players must remain in the circle and attempt to dodge the ball, while using their hands to fill a bottle with sand before the ball touches them. If playing indoors, you could substitute sand with beans, rice, or even water. If a child is hit with the ball, he or she moves out of the game. If the last child is hit, the same child continues to be "it." If the last remaining child fills a bottle without being hit, then he or she becomes the ball thrower. You might want to simply start over, asking if there are any volunteers to be "it."

Tips: When doing activities with small children, we must always consider the developmental levels, including emotional development. Slightly changing rules in order to prevent hurt feelings is certainly acceptable; the children who are "out" can be given a special helper duty, such as helping with scorekeeping.

ACTIVITY 43: Hop Little Frog

Objectives: Numeral writing and identification, fine motor skills.

Materials for each child:
- three small pebbles
- a piece of paper
- a pencil

Procedure: Place three pebbles vertically on each child's paper. Have them pretend that their pencils are frogs that will be leaping from rock to rock as they write the number three. Right-handed children should place their hands to the right of the pebbles, and left-handed children should place their hands to the left. After helping the children write a number three as their pencil frog hops from pebble to pebble, allow them to move the pebbles to different locations on their papers and play independently. Just be sure that they realize the pebbles need to be placed vertically in a row in order to make a number three.

ACTIVITY 44: Three Bee Puppet

Objectives: Numeral identification.

Materials:
- a number three cut from posterboard
- black and yellow markers
- glue
- waxed paper
- black yarn or construction paper (for antennae)

Preparation: Color the center of the three bee with black and yellow stripes. Next, waxed paper wings can be attached with glue. A head and antennae can be made with yarn, construction paper, or even pipe cleaners, if desired.

Procedure: Use Three Bee in your three activities and with the song/poem in Activity 46.

ACTIVITY 45: Three Bee - A Song or Poem

Objectives: Numeral recognition, music and rhythm skills.

Three Bee

I am a three, three, three, and I'm a bumblebee.
I can fly, fly, fly as you can see, see, see.

My favorite number is three, three, three,
and I'm as happy as can be, be, be.

ACTIVITY 46: Three Little Penguins - An Action Song or Poem

Objectives: Identification of an amount, subtraction, musical and gross motor skills.

Three Little Penguins

Three little penguins went waddle, waddle.
They waddled, and they waddled, and they waddled, waddled, waddled.
Three little penguins went waddle, waddle,
    and one penguin waddled away.

Two little penguins went flappy, flap.
They flapped, and they flapped and they flappy, flapped, flapped.
Two little penguins went flappy flap,
    and one penguin flapped away.

One little penguin went swimmy swim.
Swimmy, swim, swim, swim,
swim, swimmy swim.
One little penguin went swimmy swim,
    and then she swam away.

Zero little penguins stayed to play.
They went waddle, flap, swim far away.
Zero little penguins stayed to play.
They went waddle, flap, swim away.

Tips: Children can pretend to be penguins three at a time. Be sure to let everyone have a turn.

57 PRE-K MATH

ACTIVITY 48: Triangle Toss Game

Objectives: Identification of numeral and an amount, hand-eye coordination.

Materials:
- a large piece of cardboard or posterboard
- nine plastic bottle caps
- red, green, and blue markers or paints
- three cottage cheese containers
- sharp scissors for the teacher
- permanent marker for the teacher

Preparation: Cut the poster or cardboard to make a large triangle (approximately 2' or 3' along the base). Trace around the bottom of a cottage cheese container to make a circle in each corner of the triangle. Use sharp scissors to cut out these circles. Write a number "1" next to one hole, a "2" by another, and a "3" by the third. Place an empty cottage cheese container (without a lid) under each hole. Paint or use markers to make three red caps, three blue, and three green. Using the permanent marker, label all of the red caps with a number one, all the blue caps with a number two, and all of the green caps with a number three.

Procedure: Place all of the caps into one container, and give them to a child. Have the child stand a few feet from the triangle and attempt to throw the "1" caps in the hole labeled with a number 1, the "2" caps into the hole labeled with a number 2, and the "3" caps into the hole labeled with a number 3.

Tips: Depending on the developmental levels of the children, you may want to have them walk up and place the right bottle caps in the correct holes.

ACTIVITY 48: Magic Three Game

Objectives: Identification of numeral and an amount, estimation, and counting.

Materials:
- letters to parents
- fifty-five similar small items such as beans, candies, or marbles
- more of the same small items, enough to fill a jar completely
- three stickers for each child
- a basket
- twelve clear plastic jars

Preparation: Send home the parent letter on the following page several days in advance of this activity. Place different amounts of the small items into each jar. Include jars that contain zero items, one item, two items, etc. through ten, and one full jar. Have one jar be The Magic Three Jar, placing something special inside, such as chocolate kisses, or some glitter. Place the stickers into the basket off to the side.

Procedure: You must have twelve or fewer players. Have the children sit in a circle and give them all a jar. Have each child pass his or her jar to the person on the right. Each time a jar is passed, say the word, "Three." When you say the word, "Stop," the children can look at the items in their jars to see if they have The Magic Three Jar.

The child holding The Magic Three Jar can say, "Magic Three!" and leave the circle. Then he or she can choose three stickers from the basket and quietly play independently while the game continues.

Remove one of the jars (not The Magic Three Jar) each time a child leaves the circle. Or, if you have more than twelve children, have one child who is waiting to play replace the child who just left until everyone has a turn, and then start eliminating jars. Continue playing the game until there is only one child left. You will then be that child's partner until the child ends up holding the magic three jar and you say, "Stop." Then this child may choose three stickers from the basket.

Tips: Varying the pace of the passing develops muscle control and coordination, as well as rhythm skills. You may also choose to play music with this activity, as it is used in Musical Chairs.

LETTER TO PARENTS

Date:

Dear Parents:

This week we are focusing on the number three. Many of the songs, activities, and learning games this week will help the children to recognize, write, and count to the number three. One of these games, The Magic Three Game, requires the use of plastic jars.

If you could please send a clear, clean empty plastic jar (such as a peanut butter jar) with a lid for your child to use for our math activities, it would be greatly appreciated. We will need the jar by _____. Please contact me if you are unable to provide a jar.

Sincerely,

ACTIVITY 49: Clay Snowpeople

Objectives: Visual and tactile identification of an amount, counting, and artistic expression.

Materials:
- clay or Homemade Play Dough (See recipe below)
- small twigs
- small pebbles
- toothpicks or pipe cleaners
- long thin strips of fabric scraps

Procedure: Allow free play time with the clay, you might even want to join in the fun. Have them roll their clay into three small balls to make a head, a middle, and a bottom for a snowperson. Then stack up the three balls with the largest on the bottom. Ask the children if there are still three balls even when they are stacked on top of each other. Next, pass out all other materials and allow the children to use them with their clay making anything they wish. Allow them creative freedom to make anything they want.

Homemade Play Dough Recipe

- 2 1/2 cups of flour
- 1 cup of water
- 1 cup of salt
- Food coloring if desired

Knead for approximately ten minutes, or until you have reached the desired consistency. This recipe makes enough for four children.

ACTIVITY 50: Three Pink Flamingos: A Fingerplay and Song

Objectives: Identification of an amount, subtraction, musical, rhythm, and motor skills, and respect for the environment.

Three Pink Flamingos

Three pink flamingos
landed on a pond.
People built some houses,
and now the pond is gone.

Three pink flamingos
land in a field.
People built some buildings,
and now there is no field.

Three pink flamingos
landed by some some trees.
People came to cut the trees,
the flamingos cried, "Oh, please!"

"We need a place to build a nest!
We need a place to take a rest!
Please don't cut our trees!
We're begging you, oh please!"

The people heard the pink flamingos'
story, oh so blue.
What would you have done
if those people were YOU?

Tips: If you want to make this an action song, gather the children in a circle and have three of the children act as flamingos, running into the center of a circle and then running back. Have the rest of the children simulate building, cutting down trees, etc. All of the children can act like flamingos, balancing on one leg for the last two verses.

UNIT FIVE
The Number 4

ACTIVITY 51: Yut (YOOT) - A Game from Korea

Objectives: Counting, addition, tactile and visual identification of an amount.

Materials:
- four popsicle sticks or dice
- a marker

Preparation: This game is traditionally played with a paper game board and four wooden sticks which are flat on one side and rounded on the other. The players alternate tossing the sticks into the air and allowing them to land on the ground. Similar to a roll of the dice, the way the sticks land determines the number of moves on the board. Each player has four game pieces to move.

Procedure: If you do not wish to invent your own game board or order a traditional game of Yut, you can easily adapt this game to incorporate your resources. One version would be to take four popsicle sticks and use a marker to write different numbers on each side, making sure to include zero. Line the children up and toss the sticks into the air. You will get four numbers. For each stick, have the children do four different things. For example, if one of the sticks lands on "6," have the children jump up and down six times. If the second stick lands on "2," let the children turn around in place two times. In this version, the children will receive four sets of instructions with each toss of the sticks.

Tips: An inexpensive Yut game imported from Korea may be ordered from *The Heritage Key, Inc. Catalog.* This international children's catalog contains many games, books, toys, dolls, and other wonderful items from many cultures. Please see the Appendix for how to receive this catalog.

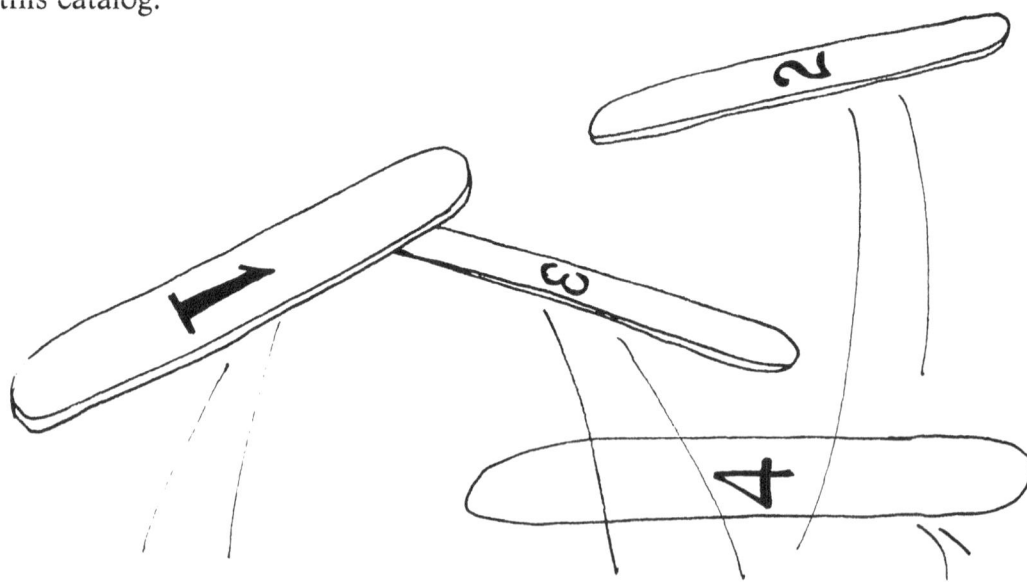

ACTIVITY 52: Mary's at the Kitchen Door - A European Nursery Rhyme

Objectives: Counting, rhythm and gross motor skills, and identification of an amount.

Mary's at the Kitchen Door

One, two, three, four,
Mary's at the kitchen door,
   Picking cherries off the floor,
Hoping they will fall no more.

Tips: Children enjoy clapping along with this rhythmic poem. Have them simulate knocking and picking up cherries, as well.

ACTIVITY 53: I Left Four Lights On In My House - A Song or Poem

Objectives: Subtraction, identification of an amount, music and rhythm skills, and environmental awareness.

I Left Four Lights On

I left four lights on in my house.
I sneak back in as quiet as a mouse.
I shut off one light, cause I care.
Leaving on lights makes dirty air!

I left three lights on in my house.
I sneak back in as quiet as a mouse.
I shut off one light, cause I care.
Leaving on lights makes dirty air!

Continue with two lights, one light, and then:

I left zero lights on in my house.
I sneak back in as quiet as a mouse.
I'm proud of me because I care.
I helped to make some cleaner air!

Tips: Before starting this song, explain that to the children that if we leave on lights, or the television when we are not using them, we make more dirty air. It's okay to use electricity, but we must not waste it.

ACTIVITY 54: Four Door

Objectives: Numeral identification, differentiating amounts, counting, and sensory exploration.

Materials:
- a cardboard box
- sharp scissors for the teacher
- several items to place inside box (see suggestions below)
- a small plastic cap or block
- a marker
- glue

Preparation: Use scissors to cut a door in the box. Glue the cap or block on as a door knob and allow the glue to dry. Draw a number four on the outside of the door with a marker.

Procedure: Select five different sets of four items for your children. Each day of Number Four Week, place four different items in the box behind the Four Door. When the children arrive each day, they can individually open the Four Door to see, feel, and count the objects, and then return them to the box for the next child to explore. To challenge the children, place four items in the box that are related in some way and have the children guess why you grouped them together. For example, place a toy car, a picture of an airplane, a stuffed animal horse, and a book about trains in the box. Have the children guess that they are all modes of transportation.

Suggested items to place in the Four Door box:
- 4 storybooks
- 4 different types of fruit to taste (try exotic fruits such as kiwi, mangos, etc.)
- 4 different writing utensils (pencil, pen, marker, chalk)
- 4 unusual feathers (a local zoo or pet store may supply these for you)
- 4 unique rocks or shells
- 4 different types of leaves
- 4 containers of fragrant items (cinnamon, peppermint, lemon slices, etc.)
- 4 differently scented candles

Tips: Depending on the items in the Four Door box, have the children use their different senses to figure out what they are. For example, with feathers, or different textures, have the children close their eyes and feel inside, using only their sense of touch. Or if there are scented candles, let the children smell inside with their eyes closed.

ACTIVITY 55: Four Count Kazoo Parade

Objectives: Counting, auditory and rhythmic identification of an amount, and musical expression.

Materials for each child:
- an empty paper towel tube
- a 4" x 4" piece of waxed paper
- a rubber band
- a ball point pen for the teacher

Preparation: Make a kazoo for each child by placing a piece of waxed paper over one end of a paper towel tube and securing it with a rubber band. Using a pen, poke two holes in the towel tube. Allow the children to decorate their kazoos with markers.

Procedure: Have a kazoo parade with the children. Count, "1-2-3-4, 1-2-3-4," and clap as they march and play their kazoos. You may wish to have them play several familiar songs as they march, or make up their own rhythms.

Tips: Allow plenty of free play time with the kazoos after the parade for the children to compose their own tunes. This exercise works well as a stress release, so you might want to schedule it for when the children have the most energy.

ACTIVITY 56: How Many Make Four? - A Fingerplay

Objectives: Counting, identification of amount, listening skills, and addition.

How Many Make Four?

One little bunny hopped around one day.
Three little bunnies said, "Come on, let's play!"
How many bunnies were there?

Children: Four!

Two little bunnies hopped around one day.
Two little bunnies said, "Come on, let's play!"
How many bunnies were there?

Children: Four!

One little bunny met another little bunny, and another little bunny, and another little bunny.
All the little bunnies said, "Come on, let's play!"
How many bunnies were there?

Children: Four!

Tips: You can either play this as a fingerplay or have the children act out the song.

ACTIVITY 57: Straw Drop

Objectives: Identification of numeral and an amount; counting, and hand-eye coordination.

Materials:
- ten plastic drinking straws
- four similar sized containers
- the numbers 1 to 4 cut from construction paper
- tape

Preparation: Tape a number cut from construction paper on the inside bottom of each container, and line up the containers in a row numerically from one to four.

Procedure: The children can take turns holding the straws at waist level and dropping the correct number of straws into each container. For example, drop three straws into the container with the three on the bottom.

Tips: This activity works best if the children play independently. Onlookers can help keep count.

ACTIVITY 58: Salt Numbers

Objectives: Numeral writing and identification.

Materials for each child:
- salt
- a paper plate
- glue

Procedure: Give each child a paper plate with some salt on it. Allow the children plenty of free time to draw in the salt using their fingers. Then show them how to use the index finger to make a large letter L in the salt. Then have them intersect that L with a straight vertical to make a number four. Ask them to squirt glue on the number fours they have made with their fingers, and have them cover the glue with salt. Allow them to dry. Collect the excess salt to save for future art use. After the salt fours have dried, you may choose to place them in plastic bags for the children to take home.

Tips: Keep one example of the Salt Four in the classroom for the children to play with.

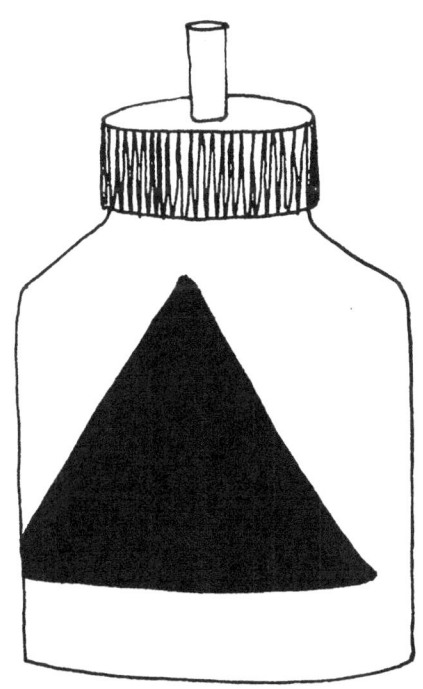
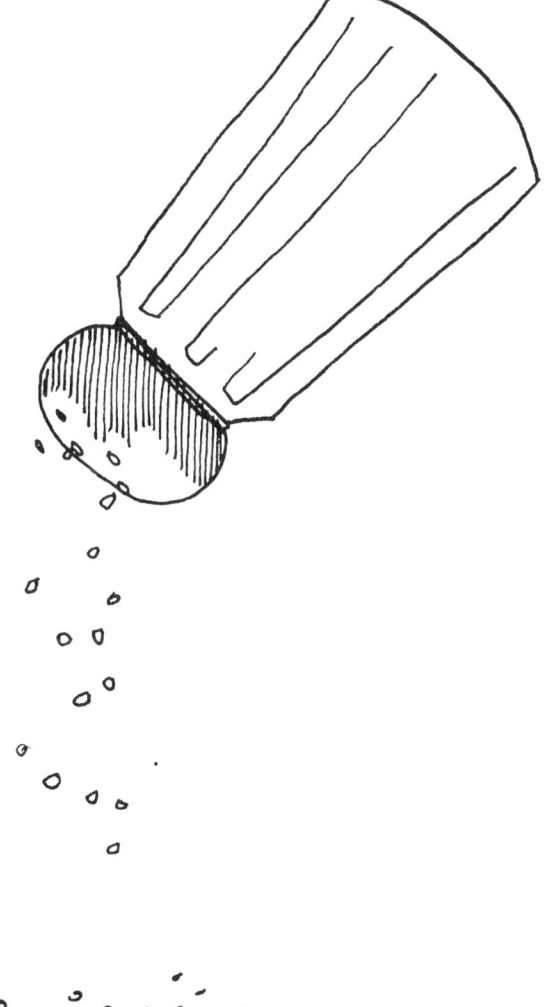

PRE-K MATH

ACTIVITY 59: Number Four Garage

Objectives: Identification of numeral and an amount, and counting.

Materials:
- scissors
- markers
- small toy vehicles with different numbers of wheels (cars, trucks, airplanes, motorcycles, etc.)
- a box for each different set of wheeled toys (a four box for cars, a two box for bicycles, etc.)

Preparation: Cut a hole in each box to make a garage door. The holes should be large enough for both the toys and a child's hand to enter. Label each box with a number which will correspond with the wheels on the toys.

Procedure: The children can play with the transportation toys and garages. Explain why the numbers are on the boxes and encourage the children to count wheels and use the corresponding garages for the toys. After playing this activity, allow the children to improvise and play freely with these materials.

ACTIVITY 60: Four Hunt

Objectives: Numeral identification, fine motor skills.

Materials for each child:
- two pipe cleaners

Procedure: Give each child two pipe cleaners. Have them bend one to resemble a capital letter L. Next, have them twist the L-shaped pipe cleaner together with the straight one to make a number four. Have the children close their eyes as you collect the fours and hide them. Allow the children to hunt for them, giving them clues along the way. Try to make sure that each child finds a four.

ACTIVITY 61: 4-legged Animal Prints

Objectives: Visual and tactile identification of an amount, counting, artistic expression, and environmental respect.

Materials:
- a variety of 4-legged plastic animal toys (dinosaurs, farm animals, etc.)
- thick poster or tempera paints spread out on trays
- a paper grocery bag for each child

Procedure: Have the children dip their toy animals' feet into the paint and decorate their paper grocery bags. Ask the children how many feet, legs, paws, or hooves each animal has. Get the children to try and name as many animals as they can with four legs.

Ask the Children: What are your grocery bags made of? Where do we get paper from? Trees have to be cut down to make paper. Are we helping to save trees by reusing our grocery bags?

Tips: When the grocery bags have dried, you can send them home, attaching the reproducible parent note on the next page to each bag with a paper clip.

PRE-K MATH

LETTER TO PARENTS

Date:

Dear Parents:

Your child is bringing home this beautifully decorated grocery bag for you to reuse again and again. To teach the children the number four, we used plastic toys of 4-legged animals to dip in paints and decorate the bags. You may wish to place another paper grocery bag inside it to make it twice as strong, and it will last even longer. Your child would be very proud to see you using the bag that has been decorated for you.

Please consider this reusable grocery bag as a reminder to reuse your grocery bags each week. You may wish to keep it in your car with other folded grocery bags inside it to help you remember to bring it on your grocery shopping trips. We can all help our earth by saving paper and preventing trees from being cut down.

Sincerely,

UNIT SIX
The Number 5

ACTIVITY 62: Istop (ee STOPE) - A Game from Turkey

Objectives: Counting, hand-eye coordination, and multiculturalism.

Materials:
- a very soft ball
- a large open area

Procedure: Five or more children may play. One child is "Ebe" (eh bay) which means "it." One child throws the ball straight up as high as possible and while the ball is in the air, the other players must run away as far as possible. Ebe will catch the ball, preferably before it hits the ground. When Ebe catches the ball, he or she shouts, "Istop," which means "stop." At this time, all the players must freeze. Picking the closest player, Ebe throws the ball at him or her. If Ebe hits that child, then they will become Ebe and a new game begins. If Ebe misses the child, then a new game begins with the same Ebe throwing the ball into the air and catching it.

Tips: Ping pong balls work well with this game. They can be thrown far and they don't cause any pain or injury. To make this game more of a learning activity, have Ebe count off the time that the ball is in the air. If it seems that the other players are too far away for Ebe to possibly hit them, allow Ebe to take five steps towards one of the players and then throw.

ACTIVITY 63: Peach Pits and Basket - A Native American Game

Objectives: Hand-eye coordination, counting, and multiculturalism.

Materials:
- five or six peach pits
- a small woven basket or bowl
- a black permanent marker for the teacher
- toothpicks

Preparation: Thoroughly wash and dry the peach pits. Use the black marker to draw a stripe on one side of each peach pit, leaving the opposite side of each pit natural colored.

Procedure: This game can be played by two or more players. Divide up into two teams. The teams alternate taking turns, one player at a time. One player holds the basket in his or her hand and gently flips the pits into the air so the other player can catch them in his or her basket. The player receives one point for each pit that lands in the basket with the black marked side facing up. You can designate points with toothpicks, and you may choose to give each child a small container to keep his or her toothpicks in, so as not to lose them.

After each child has had a turn, have each child count his or her toothpicks. Next, total the number of each team's toothpicks (points) to see which team has more. You may wish to graph the results of this game when you've finished.

Tips: The exact Native American nations which originated the games in this book are not known since many games have been, and are still being, passed on and shared at inter-tribal meetings, also known as Pow-Wows. It is known that these games existed long before the arrival of Europeans to the Americas.

Long ago, prairie grasses or real sticks were often used to keep score. The exact rules of the original game vary greatly from nation to nation. It has been known to be played by groups of men and in other nations was played by mostly women. Some nations used wooden bowls, while others used woven baskets. The pits of peaches and plums were often darkened with a hot iron on one side, and shapes such as moons and stars were painted or carved into them as a designated point system.

PRE-K MATH

ACTIVITY 64: Pizza Toss

Objectives: Visual and tactile identification of numeral and an amount, correlation of numeral with an amount, estimation, hand-eye coordination, and counting.

Materials:
- five round cardboard inserts from frozen pizzas
- crayons
- glue
- scissors
- construction paper
- tape
- an empty laundry basket

Preparation: Color the pizza cardboards red. Use construction paper to make pretend cheese, pepperoni, mushrooms, tomatoes, or other pizza toppings and glue them onto the cardboard circles. You may wish to have the children do the gluing as a cooperative project. Supply them with plenty of paint brushes and glue. As you allow the pizzas to dry completely, make a number five out of construction paper and tape it to the laundry basket.

Procedure: Have the children take turns attempting to toss the five cardboard pizzas into the basket by standing a few feet away. Younger children can stand closer. Have the children attempt to get all five pizzas in the basket. Then, have the children stack up the pizzas and count them. Are there still five? Have them spread the pizzas across the floor and count them again to see if there are still five.

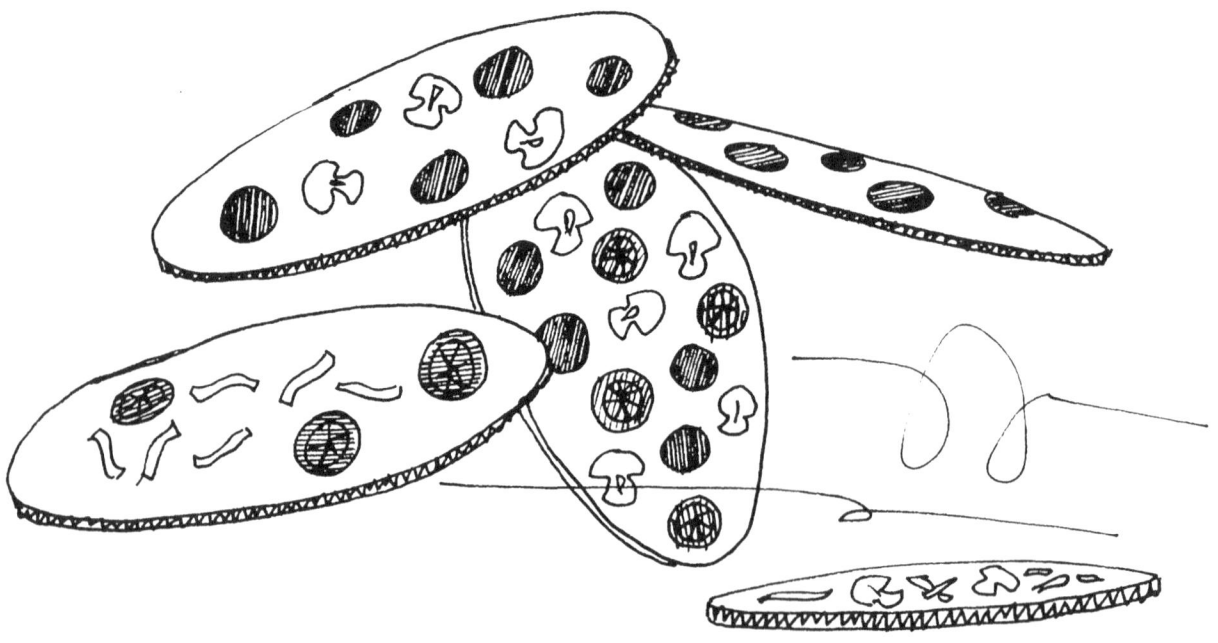

ACTIVITY 65: Silhouette Fives

Objectives: Numeral writing and identification, fine motor skills.

Materials:
- paper
- markers and pens
- a number five cut from an empty cereal box

Preparation: Make a number five silhouette in one of the following ways: tape the number five to a sunny windowpane which will reflect the five onto the floor; or attach the five to a light or lamp with a pipe cleaner. One end of the pipe cleaner can be inserted through the center of the five, and the other end can be attached to the lamp to make a silhouette on the floor.

Procedure: Have each child place a piece of paper on the number five silhouette, causing the five to appear on his or her paper. Have them trace the number five onto their paper.

Tips: Another way to do this activity would be to cut out a construction paper five for each child, and have them trace their fives individually. Once they have traced the fives, they can then color in the silhouettes, or paint them as desired.

PRE-K MATH

ACTIVITY 66: Five Trees - A Fingerplay

Objectives: Identification of an amount, addition, subtraction, fine motor skills, and environmental respect.

Five Trees

A girl climbed up one little tree,
And the tree - broke - down.
A girl climbed up two little trees,
And the trees - broke - down.
(Continue with three, four, and five trees.)

The girl stood there as sad as could be.
She cried five tears because there were no trees.
Then she thought of what she could do,
She planted five tree seeds and they grew.

The little girl planted one tree seed,
And then - it - grew.
The little girl planted two tree seeds,
And then - they - grew.
(Continue with three, four, and five tree seeds.)

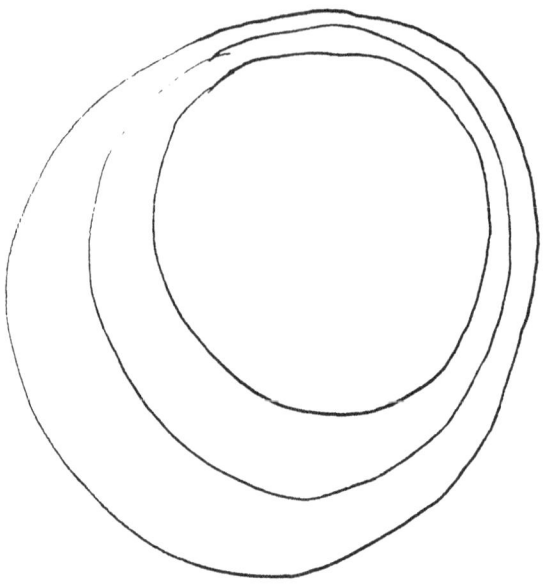

Tips: In this fingerplay, start with five fingers (trees) up. When the little girl climbs up have the index finger and middle finger of the other hand "climb up" the finger trees. When a tree breaks down, place that finger down. As the trees grow, have the fingers come back up one by one.

ACTIVITY 67: Five Little Piggies - A Fingerplay

Objectives: Identification of an amount, acceptance of differences in others, self-esteem building, and fine motor skills.

Five Little Piggies

The five little piggies are different little piggies.
They all like different things.
The five little piggies live together so happy,
And they know what friendship brings.

The five little piggies are different little piggies,
Brown, white, pink, black, and spotted too.
The five little piggies are special little piggies,
And they know that you are special, too!

Tips: Begin by saying the nursery rhyme, This Little Piggy Went to Market, using fingers instead of toes. See the Appendix for information on the book, *Fingerplays & Rhymes for Always and Sometimes,* a resource book full of creative fingerplay ideas for young children.

ACTIVITY 68: Five Fingers

Objectives: Identification of numeral and an amount, and counting.

Materials:
- pens and markers
- paper
- scissors

Procedure: Have the children trace around one of their hands. Write the numbers one through five on a piece of paper. The children may label the fingers on their hand outlines from one to five. You can assist very young children by holding onto their hands as you help them write each number. For slightly more advanced children, write the numbers by using dots, and have them connect the dots to write the numbers by themselves. Even more advanced children can look at the numbers you've written down and copy them on their own.

Tips: After each child is finished, have them cut out their hand outlines for further activities. You can call out numbers and have the children point to the fingers with the matching numeral, or just play with the cut outs freely.

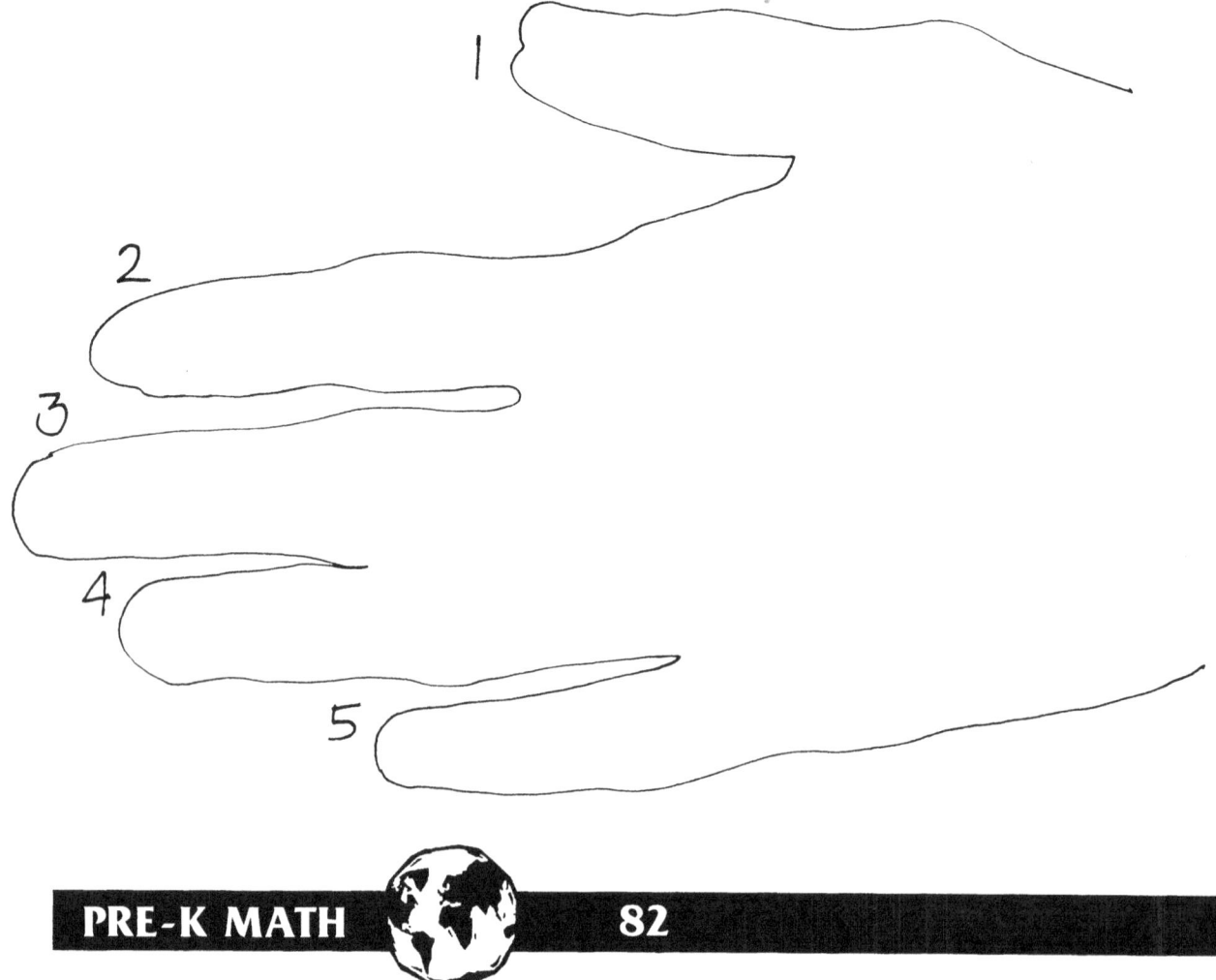

ACTIVITY 69: Dive Five Puppet

Objectives: Numeral identification.

Materials:
- scissors
- plastic or styrofoam trays
- black or blue pens
- tape
- a 12" piece of string
- shallow containers of water

Procedure: Draw a number five onto a plastic or styrofoam tray and then cut it out. Use a pen to draw a person with head down and arms overhead in a diving position onto the number five. Then, tape the string to the Dive Five. Allow free water playtime with the Dive Five and any other water play toys.

ACTIVITY 70: Dive Five - A Puppet Poem

Objectives: Identification of numeral and counting.

Dive Five

My name is Dive Five.
My name is Dive Five.
I like to dive, dive.
I like to dive, dive.
My name is Dive Five.
My name is Dive Five.
I look just like a five, five.

My name is Dive Five.
My name is Dive Five.
I like to dive, dive.
I like to dive, dive.
My name is Dive Five.
My name is Dive Five.
Watch me dive five times.
One, two, three, four, five!

Tips: This activity works well outdoors since water is used. Whenever using water for play with your children, please do not dump it down the drain after use, but rather pour it onto plants, grass, or trees. Get the children involved in and conscious of water conservation.

ACTIVITY 71: Five Ways to Get to the Store - A Fingerplay

Objectives: Identification of an amount, addition, and fine motor skills.

Five Ways to Get to the Store

I know one way to get to the store.
I can walk, walk, walk, *(have fingers walk in place)*
I can walk, walk, walk,
I know one way to get to the store.

I know two ways to get to the store.
I can run, run, run, *(have fingers run in place)*
I can walk, walk, walk, *(have fingers walk in place)*
I know two ways to get to the store.

I know three ways to get to the store.
I can skate, skate, skate, *(have fingers pretend to skate)*
I can run, run, run, *(have fingers run in place)*
I can walk, walk, walk. *(have fingers walk in place)*
I know three ways to get to the store.

I know four ways to get to the store.
I can bike, bike, bike,
I can skate, skate, skate,
I can run, run, run,
I can walk, walk, walk.
I know four ways to get to the store.

I know five ways to get to the store.
I can hop, hop, hop,
I can bike, bike, bike,
I can skate, skate, skate,
I can run, run, run,
I can walk, walk, walk.
I know five ways to get to the store.

Tips: Begin by saying, "I want to go the store, but driving my car makes the air polluted and dirty, and I want some exercise. Let's sing a song about some other ways of getting where we want to go..." You can also use this song as an action activity and have the children actually run, walk, hop, etc. as you sing.

PRE-K MATH

UNIT SEVEN
The Number 6

ACTIVITY 72: Balloon - A Game from Thailand

Objectives: Counting, identification of an amount, and multiculturalism.

Preparation: Divide six players into two teams, Intruders and Hosts. A small play area of at least 4 x 5 yards is needed. Draw lines as indicated with chalk, or mark with tape on the floor. More lines may be drawn if there are more than three players on each team. The Host team players stand at the positions marked and may move anywhere on their own lines. The first player has two lines to move on, the front entrance and the vertical center line. The Intruder team players stand at the starting point.

Procedure: The Intruder players all move into the entrance at once. Intruders must cross lines 1, 2 and 3, and return to the starting point, crossing the lines once again. If they are able to do this without being tagged by a Host, they win the game and say, "Balloon." If an Intruder is touched by a Host player, the teams switch positions and the Intruders become Hosts, and vice versa.

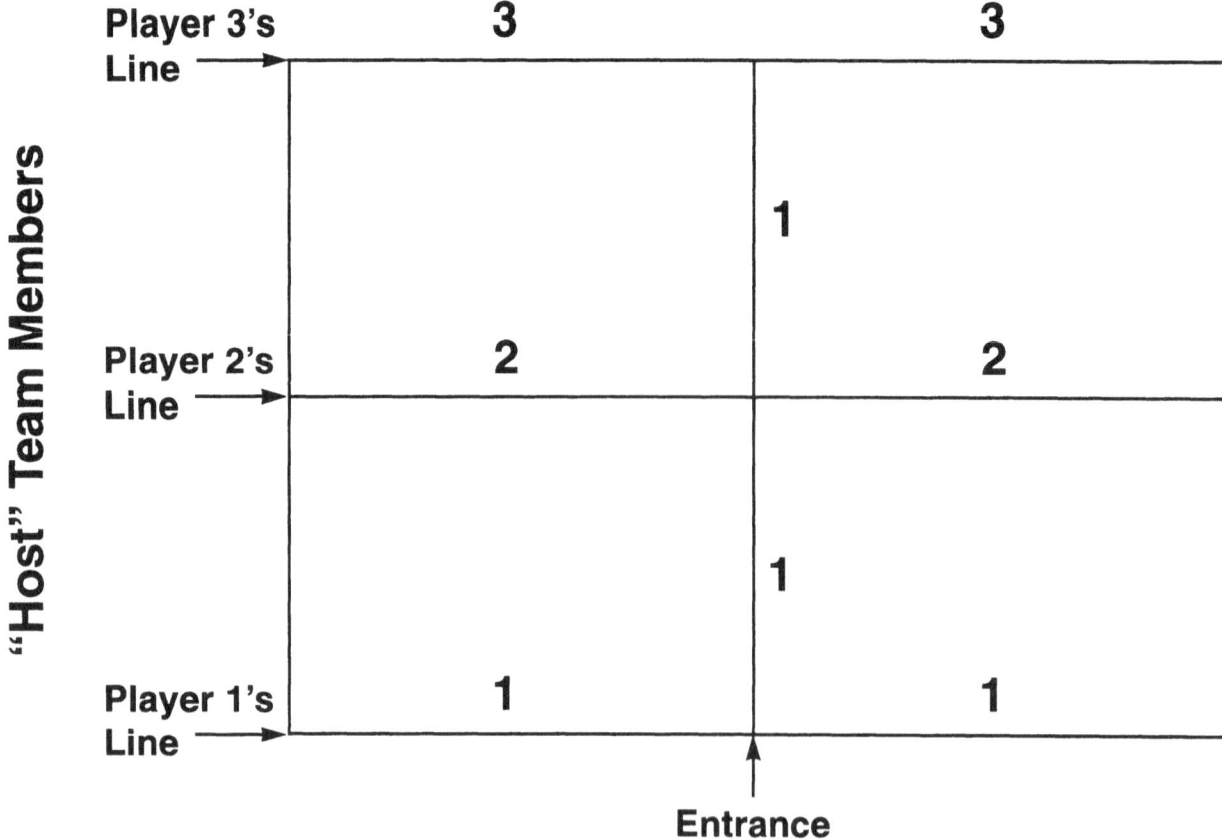

ACTIVITY 73: Six Socks in Six Sacks - A Tongue Twister

Objectives: Language and listening skills, and numeral identification.

Six Socks in Six Sacks

Six socks in six sacks.
Six socks in six sacks.
Six socks in six sacks.
Six socks in six sacks.
Six socks in six sacks.
Six socks in six sacks.

Tips: Repeat this tongue twister six times, gradually getting faster. You can also have the children hold up six fingers each time the word 'six' is spoken. See the following activity for another use for this tongue twister learning activity.

ACTIVITY 74: Six Socks in Six Sacks Game

Objectives: Identifying numeral and an amount; differentiating amounts.

Materials:
- six paper bags
- 36 clean socks
- a laundry basket
- a dark colored marker

Preparation: Have the children help roll each sock into a ball, and place the sock balls into the laundry basket. Use the marker to make a number six on the side of each bag.

Procedure: Have the children take turns attempting to throw six socks into each of the six sacks. Allow the children to stand as close as they wish.

ACTIVITY 75: How Many is Six? - A Fingerplay

Objectives: Identification of an amount, and addition.

How Many is Six?

Chorus:
How many is six?
How many is six?
Can you tell me please, how many is six?

Verses:
One over here *(hold up one finger)*
and five over here *(hold up five fingers on the other hand)*
That's one way to make six. *(to Chorus)*

Two over here *(hold up two fingers)*
and four over here *(hold up four fingers on the other hand)*
That's one way to make six. *(to Chorus)*

Three over here *(hold up three fingers)*
and three over here *(hold up three fingers on the other hand)*
That's one way to make six. *(to Chorus)*

Five over here (hold up five fingers)
and one over here (hold up one finger on the other hand)
That's one way to make six.

Tips: You may need to help young children with this fingerplay, or just let them watch and listen if it is too difficult.

ACTIVITY 76: Pigtails

Objectives: Numeral writing and identification, and fine motor skills.

Materials:
- paper
- pens and markers
- a pig pattern
- scissors for the teacher
- glue
- pipe cleaners

Preparation: Photocopy and cut out one pig for each child. Let them color them as they wish, and have them glue their pigs onto pieces of construction paper.

Procedure: Show the children how to draw a number six. You can either help them draw the sixes, or demonstrate how to form a six with a pipe cleaner. Then tell them that the six looks like a pig's tail. Have them draw a number six tail onto their pigs, or give them pipe cleaners to play with and form into sixes. They can then glue the pipe cleaners onto their pigs.

Pig Pattern

ACTIVITY 77: Six Sorting

Objectives: Identification of an amount, counting, and sorting.

Materials:
- tape
- 6 containers that can fit inside of one another, such as containers from:
  - film
  - yogurt
  - margarine
  - cottage cheese
  - a pint of ice cream
  - a can of instant coffee
  - 6 sets of six small items, such as buttons or colored paper clips (each set a different color)
  - 6 small squares of construction paper (same colors as the buttons or paper clips)

Preparation: Tape a construction paper square onto each container and write the number six. Place six items, the same color as the paper six, into each container. Then, nest the containers inside of each other with the largest on the outside.

Procedure: Have the children take turns doing this activity individually. They can take apart all of the containers and sort the items placing them in the container with the corresponding color. Then they can stack them on top of each other or nest them as they were. They will surely come up with many other ideas for using them.

ACTIVITY 78: 6-legged Rock Insects

Objectives: Visual and tactile identification of an amount, and counting.

Materials for each child:
- a rock approximately 2" in length
- acrylic paints
- a paint brush
- six pieces of black yarn 1/2" in length
- a permanent marker for the teacher

Preparation: Go rock collecting with the children. When you return, have the children wash and dry their rocks.

Procedure: Have the children paint their rocks to make their favorite insects. Allow these to dry. Next, the children can glue on the pieces of yarn to make legs. Tell them that insects have six legs, three on each side. Encourage them to count the legs by asking how many there are. Use a permanent marker to write the children's names and the date on the bottom of their insects.

ACTIVITY 79: Six Mouse Puppet and House

Objectives: Numeral identification.

Materials for Six Mouse:
- a pipe cleaner
- two small construction paper circles (eyes)
- two slightly larger construction paper circles (ears)
- a tiny pom pom (nose)
- two white twist ties (whiskers)

Materials for Six House:
- a paper grocery bag
- a marker
- scissors

Procedure: To make Six Mouse, bend the pipe cleaner to form a number six. The circular bottom portion of the six will be the mouse's body and head, and the long curved line will be the tail. Twist on the whiskers. Glue on the ears, eyes, and nose. Allow these to dry. To make Six House, draw a large number six on the paper grocery bag in blocked form. Cut out 3/4 of the inner circle of the six to make a door, leaving a small portion uncut for the hinge.

Tips: Be sure to have enough materials in case the children wish to make their own Six Mouse puppets.

ACTIVITY 80: Six Mouse Puppet Song

Objectives: Identification of numeral and an amount, and counting.

Six Mouse

Six mouse, six mouse,
lives in a six house.
Six mouse, six mouse,
where are you?
(repeat)

One, two, three, four, five, six mouse!
Come out of your little six house!

Tips: Children enjoy clapping to this song, as well as walking in time. As the children count to six in the last verse, encourage them to count on their fingers as they go.

Six Mouse Puppet Pattern (for paper)

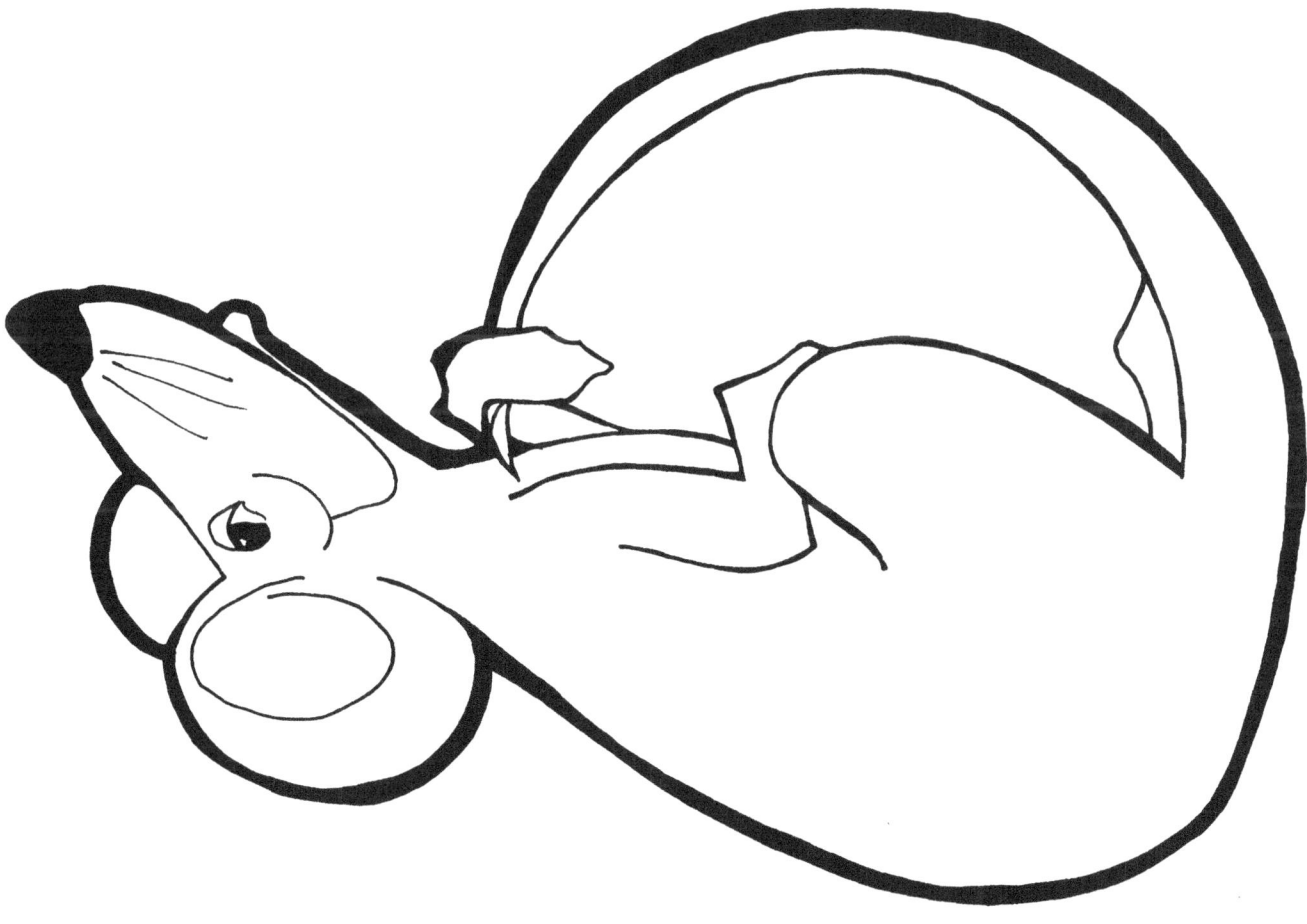

ACTIVITY 81: A Half-Dozen

Objectives: Estimation, counting, visual and tactile identification of an amount, correlation of a numeral with an amount, and sequencing.

Materials:
- a half-dozen egg carton (or a regular egg carton cut in half)
- six plastic easter eggs
- a permanent marker for the teacher

Preparation: Use the permanent marker to write a number from one to six on each egg.

Procedure: Ask the children, "Can you guess how many eggs are here without counting them?" Then allow them to count the eggs to find out. Have them place the eggs into the carton in numerical order, with the number one egg first, number two egg second, etc. Next, allow the children to use the carton and eggs freely in their dramatic play. If there are sharing difficulties, set a timer to signify when it's time to share.

Tips: Explain to the children the concept of a dozen. It may help to start off with explaining smaller groupings, such as a few, a couple, several, etc.

UNIT EIGHT
The Number 7

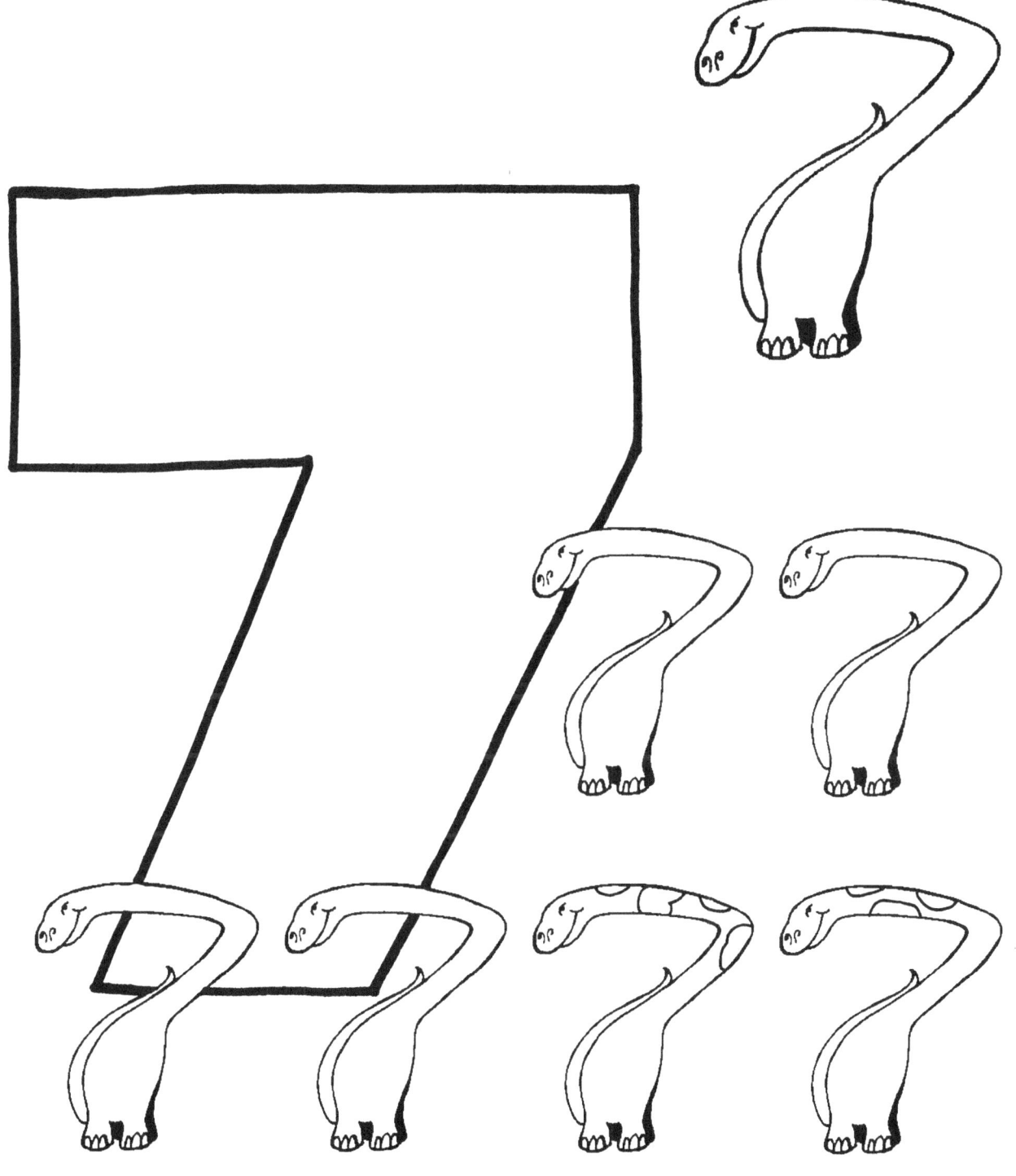

ACTIVITY 82: Bottle Cap Soccer - A Game from the Congo

Objectives: Counting, motor skills, and multiculturalism.

Materials:
- a bottle cap for each player (no metal or sharp edges)
- a marble
- two straightened paper clips
- two chewing gum wrappers (metallic paper type)
- a flat, clear playing surface indoors or outside

Preparation: Two or more players are needed. Bend the paperclips to form goals. Hang the gum wrappers on the paper clip goals. Divide the playing surface by making a center line indentation with your finger or a stick. Divide players into two teams and appoint soccer playing positions to each player, including the goalie position.

Procedure: The players can use their bottle caps to flick or bump the marble forward as if they had kicked the ball in a soccer game. After a goal is scored by one team, the marble is rolled to the other team. The adult watching can help keep track of how many attempts were made and how many actual goals were scored by each side. You may etch a scoreboard into the sand. You may also wish to graph these results for each team. The first team to reach seven goals is the winning team.

Tips: Since marbles will be used, you may need to make borders, such as rows of wooden blocks or cardboard boxes, so they don't roll away. Soccer is a very popular sport in many parts of the Congo as well as throughout the world.

ACTIVITY 83: Hop Around the Days of the Week - A Game from Cuba

Objectives: Counting, gross motor skills, and multiculturalism.

Materials:
- a piece of chalk
- a sidewalk or concrete outdoor playing surface, free from traffic

Procedure: Draw seven connecting squares in the shape of an arc. Write the days of the week, one in each square. The children can hop on one or two feet (depending on developmental levels) from day to day while singing or saying the days of the week. You may place a small number by each day so that they can associate the number seven with how many days there are in one week.

Tips: This Cuban game is similar to the game of Hopscotch played in the United States. However, in Cuba rubber heels from shoes are tossed from place to place, rather than pebbles.

ACTIVITY 84: Number Seven Touch and Guess

Objectives: Counting, tactile numeral identification, and numeral writing.

Materials:
- glue
- a cardboard box with a hole cut out
- two pipe cleaners
- two frozen popsicle sticks
- two twigs
- two toothpicks
- two drinking straws
- two cocktail straws
- two tongue depressors (available at large pharmacies)
- scissors for the teacher

Preparation: Use scissors to cut one of each pipe cleaner, straw, etc. in half, so you will have one long and one short of each. When breaking the twigs and tongue depressors, make sure to use an emery board to smooth any rough edges. Then glue the above listed items (in the shape of seven number sevens) in various locations inside the box. Allow these to dry.

Procedure: Have each child place his or her hand into the box without peeking in. Let them feel all the number sevens inside. Ask them to identify what they are feeling, either what number, or what the numbers are made out of. After everyone has had a turn, you can open the box and show them all the sevens inside.

Tips: Please see the Appendix for information on The National Federation of the Blind. Contact this organization for free and inexpensive learning materials which help introduce the children to disabilities and blindness. There is also a listing for an easy to use book of Sign Language. Young children are fascinated with this language, and will probably pick it up in no time.

ACTIVITY 85: Seven Globs of Trash - A Fingerplay and Song

Objectives: Identification of a numeral, subtraction, and environmental respect for the oceans.

Seven Globs of Trash

Seven globs of trash, littered on the beach.
I can pick one up, it just takes a little reach.

Six globs of trash, littered on the beach.
I can pick one up, it just takes a little reach.
(Repeat for five, four, three, two, and one)

Zero globs of trash, littered on the beach.
I picked them up, it just took a little reach.

Using beaches for our trash would be so very mean.
I keep ocean creatures happy by keeping beaches clean.

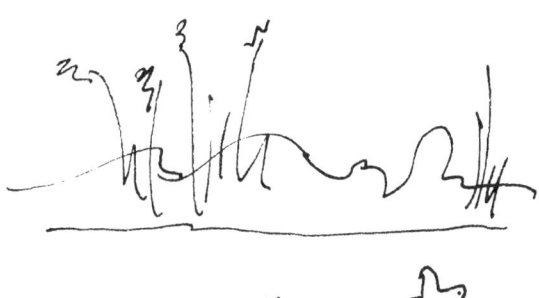

Ask the Children: What types of animals live in the ocean, and how do you think trash affects them?

Tips: The plastic rings which hold soda cans together should be broken before they are thrown away. The rings can wrap around the necks of many sea creatures and birds. Have the children ask their parents to save these plastic rings, and you can cut them up and use them for various activities in the classroom.

ACTIVITY 86: Estimation Game

Objectives: Estimation, visual and tactile identification of an amount, correlation of numeral with an amount.

Materials:
- a large piece of paper
- a marker
- three empty, clear plastic containers (peanut butter jars work well)
- seven seeds
- seven milk or juice lids
- seven items which are slightly larger (building blocks, small toy cars, etc.)

Preparation: Put the seeds, lids, and building blocks into the three clear containers. Write a large number seven on the back of a large piece of paper. The front of the paper will be for writing down the children's estimates.

Procedure: Hold up the first jar and ask the children to guess how many items are in it. Write down the children's estimates. Hold up the second jar and again have the children estimate, recording their guesses. Continue with the third jar. Next, dump out each jar and have the children help you as you count each separate group of items. Show the children the paper with the number seven drawn on it after counting each group of items. The children will be amazed to discover that all the jars contained seven items. Allow them to use the materials on their own for investigation and play.

ACTIVITY 87: Book of Seven

Objectives: Visual identification of a numeral, tactile identification of an amount, counting, and correlation of numeral with an amount.

Materials:
- construction paper (eight 5" x 5" sheets for each child)
- non-toxic glue, or rubber cement
- a stapler for the teacher
- seven different types of small items, such as:
    - buttons
    - small leaves
    - pebbles
    - small flowers
    - sequins
    - stickers
    - paper clips
    - seeds

Procedure: Give each child seven leaves. Have them glue the seven leaves to one of their 5" x 5" pieces of construction paper. Then, hand out seven sequins, repeating until each child has seven pages with seven items on each page. Allow the pages to dry. Staple together each child's book adding a blank page for the cover. The children can draw a large number seven on their book covers and decorate them as they wish.

Tips: This book can also be made a few pages per day if desired.

ACTIVITY 88: Fishing for Sevens

Objectives: Tactile and visual numeral identification.

Materials:
- a large unbreakable bowl
- pipe cleaners
- scissors

Preparation: Cut several pipe cleaners in half and bend each half into a number from zero to nine, including several number sevens. Place all of the numbers into the bowl. Use fewer numbers for children who are younger or at earlier levels of development.

Procedure: Give each child a pipe cleaner and have him or her bend it to make a number seven-shaped fishing pole. Then have the children take turns trying to hook the numbers in the bowl onto their seven fishing poles, trying to get as many sevens as possible. If any other number is caught, it must be thrown back into the bowl. Only sevens can be kept. After each child has a turn, allow free play with these items.

Tips: Rather than using different numbers in the bowl, you can fill the bowl with number sevens for children who cannot easily differentiate numbers.

ACTIVITY 89: Seven Snacks

Objectives: Numeral identification.

Suggestions: Serve bread sticks for a snack. The bread sticks can be connected with cream cheese or peanut butter to form number sevens. Additional cream cheese or peanut butter may be served to use for dipping the bread sticks. You could also spread peanut butter in the form of the number seven on pieces of bread for the children to enjoy.

ACTIVITY 90: Sevenocchio Puppet

Objectives: Numeral identification.

Materials for each child:
- a tongue depressor
- a frozen popsicle stick
- putty adhesive
- markers
- yarn
- glue

Preparation: Cut the popsicle sticks in half, making sure that there are no rough edges.

Procedure: Have the children use markers to draw the profile of a face at the top of their tongue depressors (no nose is necessary yet.) They can glue on yarn for hair if desired. Allow these puppets to dry. Next, each child can use putty adhesive to attach their halved popsicle sticks as noses for their puppets. If you do not wish to use these puppets for the puppet show in the following activity, the children can use glue for the noses, instead. The puppets will now be in the shape of number sevens.

Tips: You can use this opportunity to read or tell the story of *Pinnochio* to the children, reinforcing the importance of honesty. Another picture book for very young children on this subject is *Fibber E. Frog,* a story about a frog whose low self-esteem prompts him to tell fibs and tell tall tales to make friends. Please see the Appendix for more information on this title.

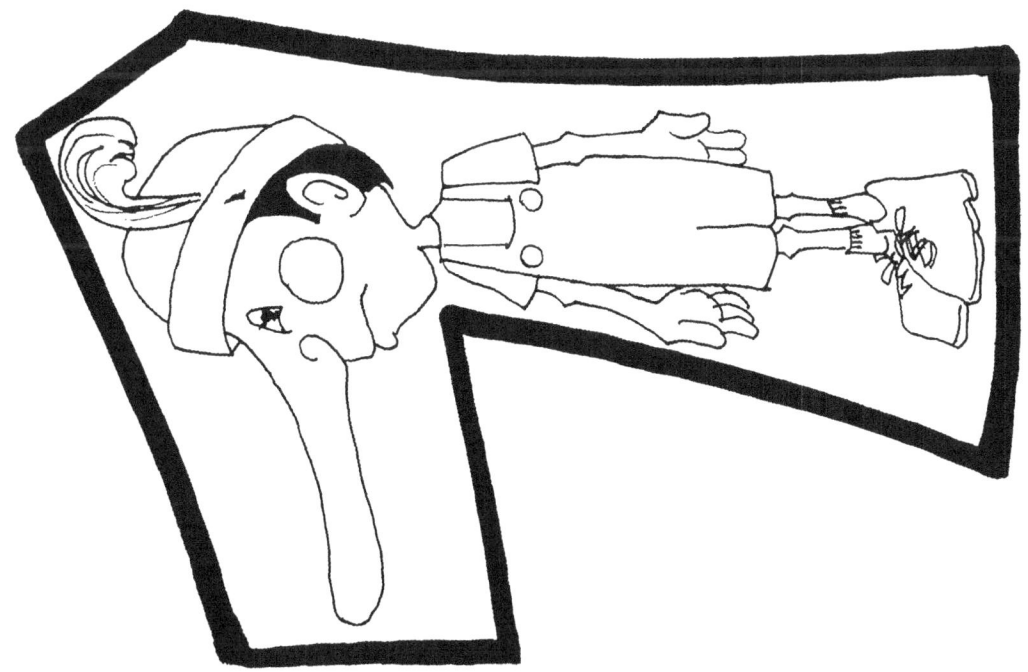

ACTIVITY 91: Sevenocchio - A Puppet Show

Objectives: Identifying a numeral and an amount, counting, estimating, and dramatic play.

Preparation: Remove the frozen popsicle stick nose from one of the puppets. Set up several groups of seven items around the room, and a few groups with other amounts. For example, in one corner place seven toys, put seven pieces of chalk on the chalkboard, put seven chairs in a row, and place four dolls together.

Puppet Show: Introduce the puppet as Sevenocchio. The puppet then says, "Hi kids! I am Sevenocchio! Every time I count to seven, something magical happens to me - I become a number seven. Let's look around the room together and see if we can count seven of something, and you can watch me turn into a number seven."

Whenever Sevenocchio counts seven of something, his nose grows turning him into a number seven. If he counts and there are less than seven items, his nose will not grow.

Take the children around the room and count each group of items. Whenever there is a group of seven items, slowly slide the nose along the puppet's face to make the nose appear to be growing. To make the nose get smaller again, have the children say, "Seven, seven go away!"

Sevenocchio decides he likes looking like a seven and thinks he'd like to stay that way. Tell the children they have to shout, "Seven!" seven times and then Sevenocchio will stay a number seven. Hold up your fingers as the children say, "Seven!" in order to help them count how many times they have said it. Then use putty adhesive to reattach Sevenocchio's nose.

Tips: Have the children play freely with their own Sevenocchio puppets. They might come up with some fairytales of their own!

UNIT NINE
The Number 8

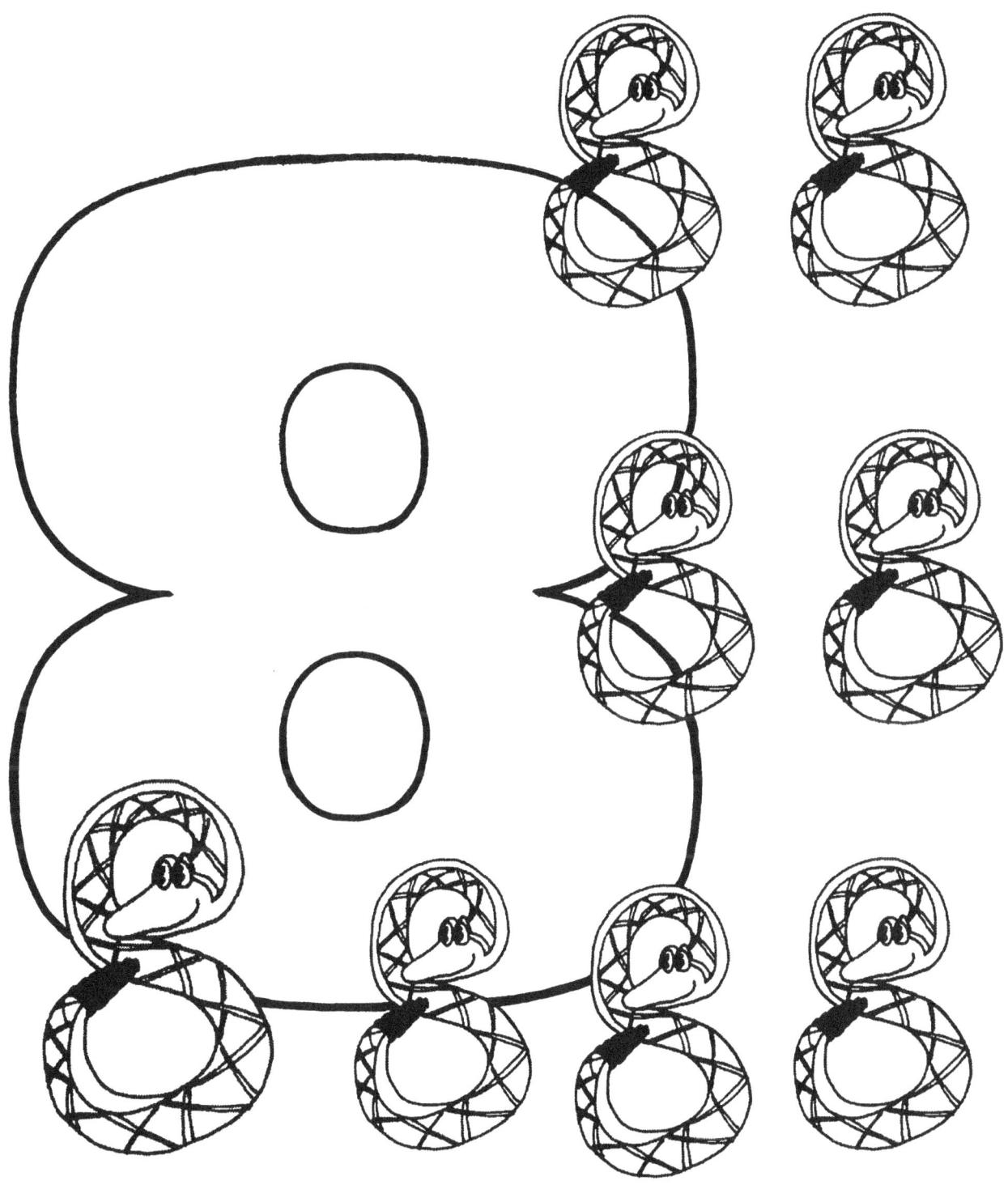

ACTIVITY 92: Juego del Panuelo (WAYgo del PANyuWAYlo) - A Game from Cuba

Objectives: Counting, identification of an amount, gross motor skills, and multiculturalism.

Materials:
- a handkerchief or scarf

Procedure: This game is similar to the game Duck, Duck, Goose. The children sit in a circle, and one child who is "it" walks around the outside of the circle carrying a handkerchief. When whoever is "it" drops the handkerchief behind a sitting child, that child picks up the handkerchief and chases "it." If "it" reaches the empty spot in the circle first, then "it" sits in that spot and the child holding the handkerchief is now "it." But, if the child holding the handkerchief catches "it," then "it" must sit in the middle of the circle, and the child with the handkerchief is "it." One by one, children will be eliminated and sitting in the middle of the circle. When a child who is "it" is eliminated, you might want to say, "Now you get to sit in the middle," to make it sound exciting, not like a loss.

Tips: To use math concepts within this game, ask the children to count how many children are in the circle. When children start entering the middle of the circle, ask them to count how many are in the middle, and how many are left in the circle, using subtraction skills. When there are eight children in the middle, the game is over. Or simply have the child who is "it" count children as they go by before dropping the handkerchief.

ACTIVITY 93: Eight Obstacle Course

Objectives: Sensory identification of an amount, visual identification of a numeral, correlation of numeral with an amount, gross motor skills, and counting.

Materials:
- two hula hoops
- eight cardboard boxes (large enough for the children to crawl through)
- eight shoeboxes with lids
- a marker
- sidewalk chalk

Preparation: Open both ends of each cardboard box, place open ends together, and write a number from one to eight on the outside and on the inside bottom of each box. Write a number from one to eight on each shoebox lid and on the inside of each shoe box. Use sidewalk chalk to draw a large number eight on the concrete or sidewalk.

Procedure: Set up your obstacle course outdoors as your space and safety conditions will permit. Place the hula hoops together to resemble a number eight for the children to hop over without stepping on. Open both ends of each of the cardboard boxes to form several tunnels, or one long maze for the children to climb through. Set up the shoeboxes and lids so that the children can hop from box to box and from lid to lid, counting as they hop. Play follow the leader as you all move through the course. Allow each child the chance to be the leader.

Tips: Make sure the children are under constant supervision with this activity. After everyone has had a turn as leader, allow the children to change around the obstacle course as they desire.

ACTIVITY 94: Eight Circle Trace

Objectives: Identification of a numeral and an amount, fine motor skills, and artistic expression.

Materials:
- markers
- crayons
- paints
- large pieces of paper
- coins of different diameters
- many different sized lids such as those from:
    - syrup bottles
    - soda (plastic bottle)
    - orange juice
    - milk
    - cottage cheese
    - whipped topping
    - margarine
    - yogurt

Procedure: Have the children make beautiful designs on their papers by tracing their circles. Encourage counting by asking how many circles they have drawn. Many of the finished drawings will resemble number eights. Give the children as much paper as they want for this activity. After they have finished, have them write or count how many eights they can find.

Tips: This activity works well when music is played in the background. For dramatic results, bring in several different types of music from classical to rock, including music from other countries, and see what effect the music has on the art styles. See Activity 111 for a related art project.

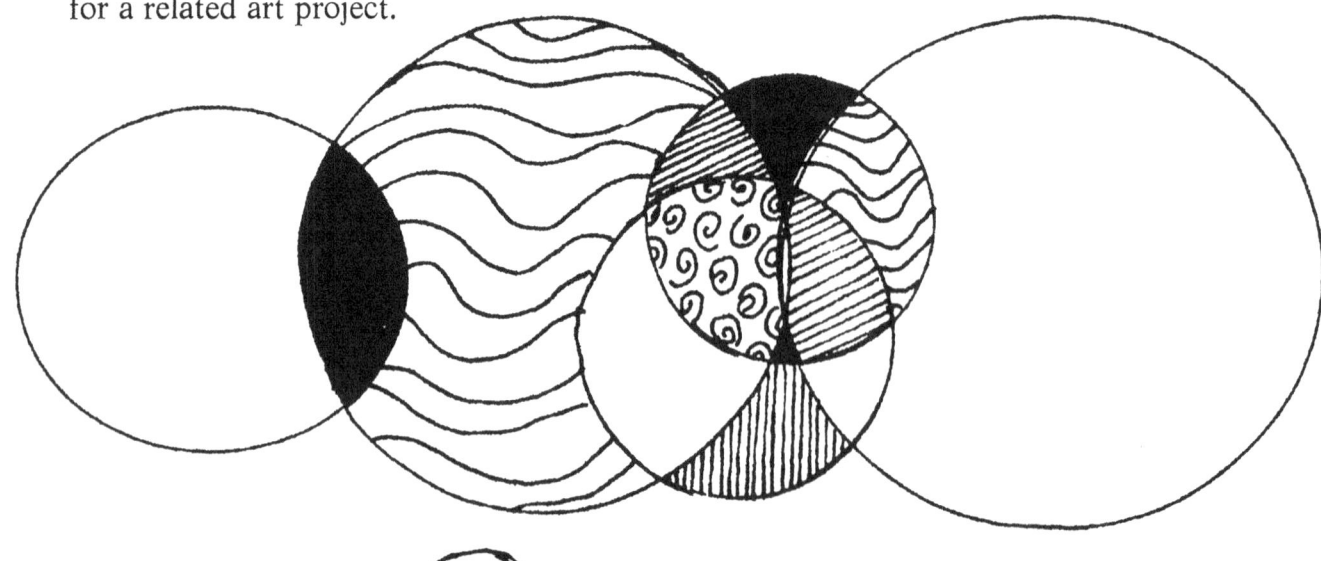

ACTIVITY 95: Eight Little Balls Were Rolling - A Fingerplay and Song

Objectives: Identification of an amount, counting, subtraction, addition, and motor skills.

Eight Little Balls Were Rolling

Eight little balls were rolling, rolling.
Eight little balls at play.
Eight little balls were rolling, rolling.
One ball rolled away.

Seven little balls were rolling, rolling.
Seven little balls at play.
Seven little balls were rolling, rolling.
One ball rolled away.
(Then six, five, four, three, two, and one)

Zero little balls were rolling, rolling.
Zero little balls at play.
Zero little balls were rolling, rolling.
Come back here to stay!

Eight little balls were bouncing, bouncing.
Eight little balls at play.
Eight little balls were bouncing, bouncing.
Now they're here to stay!

One, two, three, four, five, six, seven, eight!

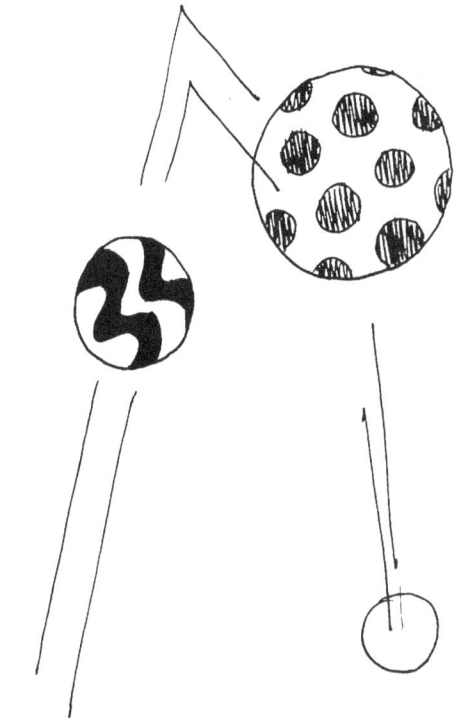

Tips: Have the children count on their fingers along with the song, and use hand motions to simulate rolling. The children can jump up and down when the balls are bouncing, and have them bounce and count for the last line. See the following activity for more suggestions to accompany this fingerplay.

ACTIVITY 96: Rolling Balls Subtraction

Objectives: Subtraction, visual identification of an amount, rhythm skills.

Materials:
- a long, empty cardboard tube (from wrapping paper or several paper towel tubes taped together)
- a piece of foam pad or another surface on which balls will not roll easily
- eight small super bounce balls
- a bucket
- a small table
- masking tape

Preparation: Place the foam pad on a small table. Set the eight super bounce balls on the pad. Place the bucket on the floor next to the table. Use masking tape to attach the top of the cardboard tube to the table. Angle the tube away from the table like a slide and tape the bottom end of the tube to the bucket. When a ball is put into the top of the tube, it should roll down the tube and land in the bucket.

Procedure: Use the fingerplay game in the preceding activity and have the balls go from the sponge surface down the cardboard tube, subtracting them one by one. Let the children take turns practicing dropping the balls down the tube, trying to match rhythm with the words. When you have finished, allow the children to use the materials on their own in pairs or individually.

Tips: A timer with a bell or an alarm clock may be set to determine when it's time to share. Tell the children how many minutes you will set the timer for, showing them yet another way numbers are important in life.

PRE-K MATH

ACTIVITY 97: Number Eight Super Hero Masks

Objectives: Visual and tactile numeral identification, numeral writing, counting, and dramatic play.

Materials:
- empty cereal and cracker boxes or posterboard
- markers
- scissors
- a hole punch
- yarn (one 25" piece and two 10" pieces for each child)
- tape

Preparation: Draw a 3" x 6" number eight on a cereal box panel or posterboard for each child. You may wish to cut out the centers of the eights for the children, or have them cut out the circles themselves. Wrap a small piece of tape around one end of each 25" piece of yarn for easy threading and knot the other ends. Knot one end of each 10" piece of yarn.

Procedure: Have the children cut out centers of their number eights and color them with markers. Have them pretend that their markers are horses or cars on a race track to practice writing number eights in a fun way. Next, punch eight holes in each child's eight, counting aloud with each hole punch. Have them lace up the holes with their 25" pieces of yarn. Using the two 10" pieces of yarn, insert each of these into the top and bottom holes of the eight. Then, turned sideways, the eights become hero masks that can be tied behind the children's heads.

Tips: In addition to the masks, you may wish to add super hero capes for dramatic play. Old graduation gowns work nicely, or any large pieces of cloth.

Pattern for Number Eight Super Hero

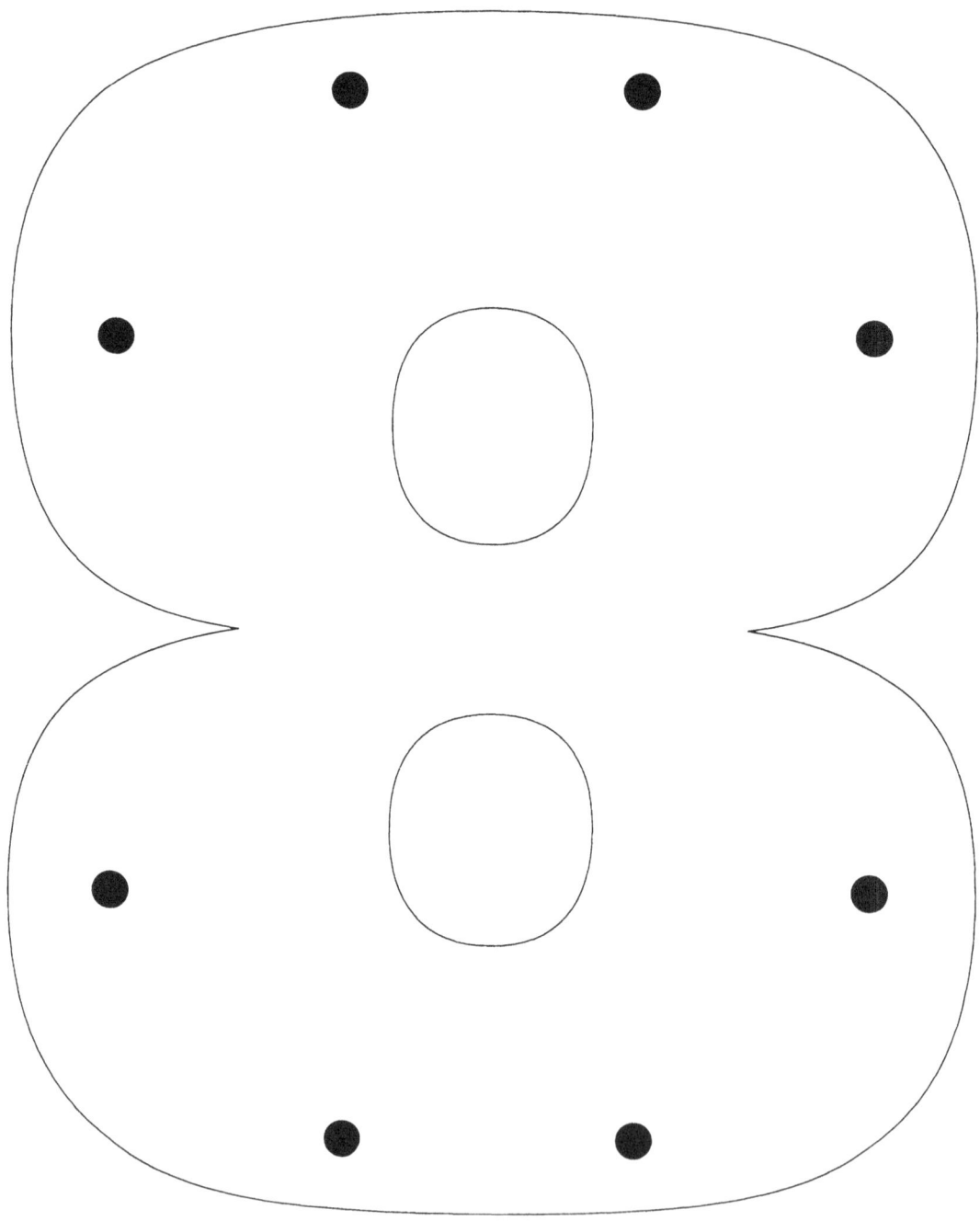

ACTIVITY 98: Eight O'Clock Bedtime - A Song

Objectives: Counting, correlation of numerals with time, music and rhythm skills.

Eight O'Clock Bedtime

Chorus:
At eight o'clock, at eight o'clock,
My bedtime is at eight o'clock.
At eight o'clock, at eight o'clock,
My bedtime is at eight o'clock.

Verse:
I get my jammies, and brush my teeth.
May I have a story, please?
How about a kiss and a hug for me?
'Cause my bedtime's eight o'clock.
(To chorus)

One,
　two,
　　three,
　　　four,
　　　　five,
　　　　　six,
　　　　　　seven,
　　　　　　　eight -
time - for - bed!

Tips: Have the children clap as they sing or say the last line, then have them snore, shut their eyes, and tilt their heads to the side.

ACTIVITY 99: Number Eight Snacks

Objectives: Numeral identification and counting.

Materials:
- two mini bagels per child
- peanut butter
- raisins
- plastic knives

Suggestions: Mini bagels can be sliced into halves. Give each child two halves and ask them to form a number eight. Next, give each child a plastic knife, a small portion of peanut butter, and some raisins. The children can then spread peanut butter on their bagels and count out eight of their raisins to place on their Number Eight Snacks if they wish. An alternative to bagels would be pretzels. Give each child eight pretzels and see if they can figure out how to make them look like eights. Milk goes well with both of these nutritious snacks.

UNIT TEN
The Number 9

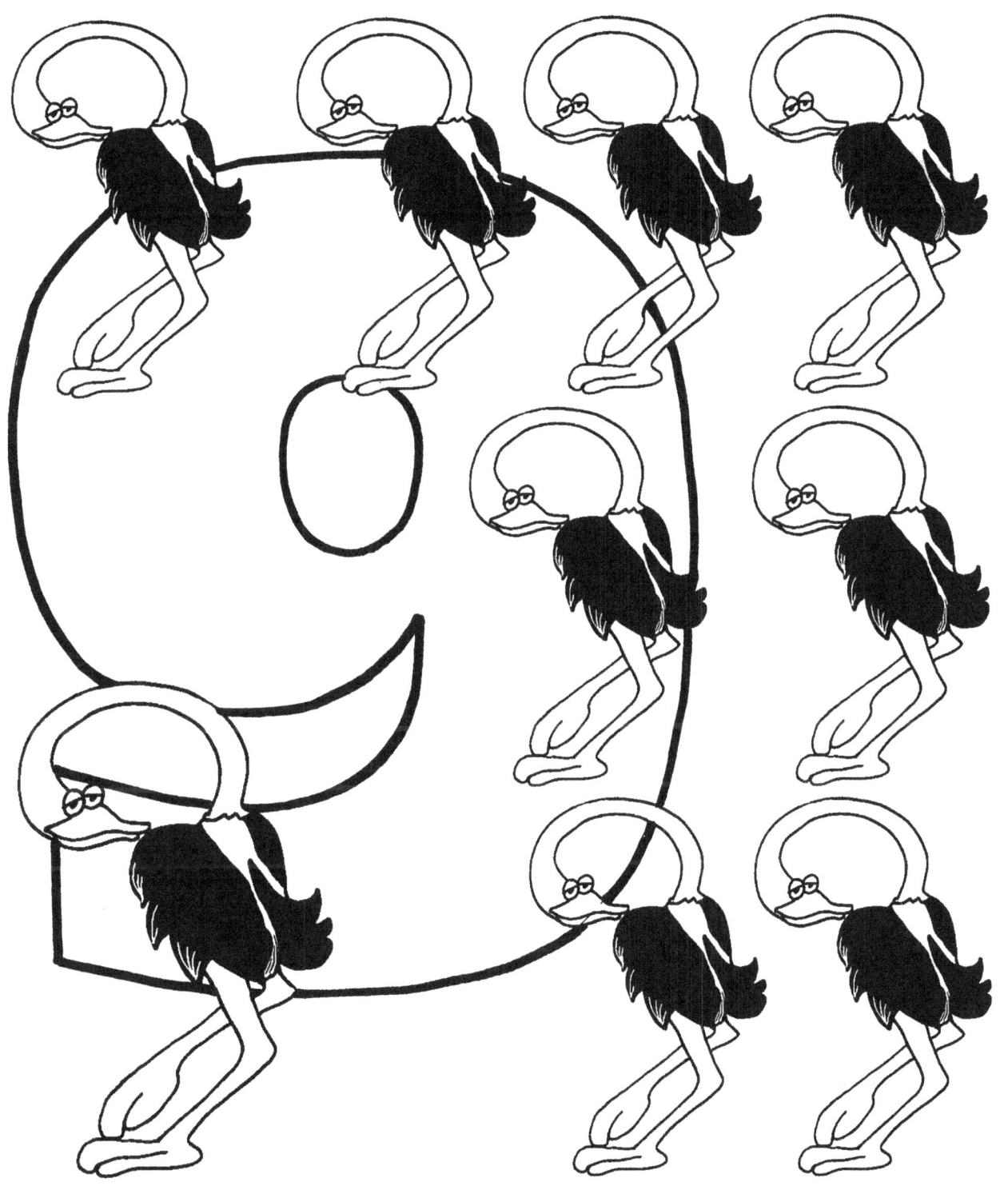

ACTIVITY 100: A Pallonate (ah PAHlo NAHtay) - A Game from Italy

Objectives: Counting, gross motor skills, hand-eye coordination, and multiculturalism.

Materials:
- a foam or sponge ball
- a large wall

Procedure: This game can be played inside or outside against any large wall. One child gets the ball and the other children must stand up against the wall. The child with the ball attempts to hit the other players and "tag" them out. The children can move from side to side slightly (being careful not to bump into anyone else) and duck down to avoid being hit with the ball. Once tagged out, a child must leave the wall. If the thrower misses and does not hit any children three times in a row, then a new game starts with a different thrower. If, however, the thrower tags out everyone, they have the option to be the thrower in the next game.

Expanding Upon Math Concepts: Count and keep track of how many children there are against the wall. You can keep a tally of how many throws it takes to tag every child. You may wish to arrange the game so that each child has a chance to throw the ball for a certain length of time. You can later make a graph showing how many throws each child made and how many children were tagged during each child's turn.

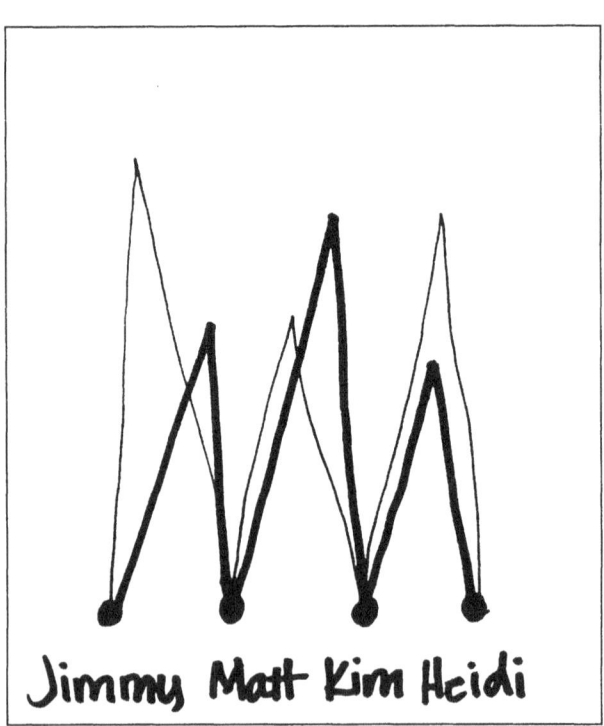

Tips: Please use sensitivity regarding the feelings of young children. Leaving the game should not be equated with losing. You might try to find a special duty, such as keeping score, for the children as they are moved out.

ACTIVITY 101: Rock-n-Roll Nine Puppet

Objectives: Numeral identification.

Materials:
- construction paper
- markers
- scissors
- half-inch scraps of yarn
- glue
- a 14" piece of yarn
- a hole punch

Preparation: Stencil a six-inch number nine onto construction paper and then cut it out. Use markers to draw sunglasses, a mouth, and a small guitar. Glue on the scraps of yarn for hair. Punch a hole in the top of the nine and thread a 14" piece of yarn through the hole and tie a knot.

Procedure: Use this puppet in any of your number nine activities and with the song in Activity 102. These are very easy to make, so consider having the children make their own to sing along. You could bring in several cassettes of rock music, or obtain some cassettes from your library of music from various countries for the children.

Tips: Please see the Appendix for listings of several musical cassettes that feature songs from various countries and cultures.

ACTIVITY 102: Rock-n-Roll Nine - A Puppet Song

Objectives: Identification of numeral, and music and rhythm skills.

Rock-n-Roll Nine

Rock-n-roll nine,
Rock-n-roll nine,
You're doin' so fine.
Rock-n-roll nine.

I see that little nine,
Rocking all the time.
He can really shine,
He's a rock-n-roll nine.

Rock-n-roll nine,
Rock-n-roll nine,
You're doin' so fine.
Rock-n-roll nine.

ACTIVITY 103: Silver Nine

Objectives: Numeral identification, fine motor skills, and observational skills.

Materials:
- scraps of aluminum foil

Procedure: Give each child a piece of foil similar in size. Have them roll the foil to make a narrow strip and then bend the strip to form a number nine. You can place these on the bulletin board, or have the children try and find places to hang their nines around the room. If they can find doorknobs, coat hooks, etc., to hang their Silver Nine decorations, they will remember which way the nine faces, as opposed to sixes. After the children have manipulated their nines for a while, have them turn them upside down and ask them what they find.

Tips: You can ask parents to save any of their clean aluminum scraps for your activities. This activity also works well with pipe cleaners, or even playdough. Please see Activity 50 for an easy recipe which you can use to make your own Homemade Play Dough.

ACTIVITY 104: What's the Magic Number?

Objectives: Numeral recognition, fine motor skills, and sensory exploration.

Materials for Each Child:
- a light-colored construction paper nine
- a white sheet of typing paper
- transparent tape
- several large crayons

Preparation: Remove the paper from all of the crayons you will be using. Place a construction paper nine and a piece of typing paper over it at each child's place without letting them see. Tape down the corners of each piece of typing paper.

Procedure: Call the children to the table and give them each several crayons. Tell them that a magic number will appear on their papers if they rub their crayons (horizontally) over their papers. Have them guess what the magic number is. Then have them guess why the number appeared on their papers. After they are through, remove the tape and lift the papers to expose the construction paper nines.

Tips: Crayon rubbings also work well with leaves for various art projects. Consider setting up a table of surprise rubbings for the children, hiding bits of grass, leaves, coins, animals cut from construction paper, etc.

ACTIVITY 105: Hop Around a Nine

Objectives: Counting, gross motor skills, identification of numeral and an amount, and correlation of numeral with an amount.

Materials:
- nine non-slip bathtub decals
- putty adhesive

Preparation: Place the decals on the floor approximately 10" apart from one another in the shape of the number nine. You could use a permanent marker to write the numbers from one to nine on the decals if you wish. Adhere the decals to the floor with several small pieces of putty adhesive on the bottom of each one.

Procedure: Have the children take turns hopping on the decals, moving around the nine from the bottom of it to the top. Older children can attempt to hop on one foot.

Tips: If you cannot find bathtub decals, this activity works just as well with circles made out of masking tape on the floor.

ACTIVITY 106: Recycle - A Song

Objectives: Addition, identification of an amount, environmental respect, and music and rhythm skills.

Recycle

Chorus:
Recycle your trash, don't throw it all away.
Recycle your trash, so we have room to play.
Recycle your trash, don't throw it all away,
or it will stay forever and a day.

Verses:
I drank five bottles of milk one day.
My friend said, "Don't throw those bottles away!"
So I took five bottles right to a place
where they recycle garbage waste. *(To Chorus)*

I drank four bottles of juice one day.
My mom said, "Don't throw those bottles away!"
I took four bottles right to a place
where they recycle garbage waste. *(To Chorus)*

Ask the Children: Five milk bottles and four juice bottles were recycled. How many bottles were recycled all together? The children can use real empty juice and milk containers and their fingers to add.

ACTIVITY 107: Show Me Nine - A Clapping Rhythm Poem

Objectives: Addition, identification of an amount, and music and rhythm skills

Show Me Nine

Chorus:
Show me nine.
Show, show me nine.
Show me nine.
Show, show me nine.

Verses:
Five and four. Five and four.
Five and four make nine.
Five and four make nine.

Six and three. Six and three.
Six and three make nine.
Six and three make nine.

Seven and two. Seven and two.
Seven and two make nine.
Seven and two make nine.

Eight and one. Eight and one.
Eight and one make nine.
Eight and one make nine.

Tips: Have the children mimic you as you hold up the correct number of fingers for each verse.

UNIT ELEVEN
The Number 10

ACTIVITY 108: Gioco delle Figurine (jOgo DEHLah FihgooDEEnah) - A Game from Italy

Objectives: Counting, addition, subtraction, and hand-eye coordination.

Materials:
- several decks of old playing cards
- a table, or any flat raised surface

Procedure: Give each child a stack of ten cards, or have one child pass out the cards evenly so that each player gets the same amount. Each child takes a turn placing one of his or her cards on the table and flicking it off onto the floor, using a sideways flick with the tip of the index finger. If the card touches or lands on top of any of the other cards on the floor, they get to keep them. The object is to collect as many cards as possible. When the game is over (whenever someone runs out of cards), each remaining child can count how many cards he or she has left. Did they end up with more or less than they started with?

Tips: This game is traditionally played with soccer player trading cards. The children collect these cards and save their most prized ones in an album. With the cards that are less special, they play this game in hopes of obtaining some new ones. Many children became very skilled at playing this trading game.

ACTIVITY 109: Varanasi Numbers - A Game from India

Objectives: Numeral writing, visual and auditory identification of a numeral, and listening skills.

Materials:
- two small chalkboards
- two pieces of chalk

Procedure: Two children can play at a time. Each child writes the numbers from 0-10 down the left side of his or her chalkboard in a column. The child who goes first picks any number from one to ten and draws it on his or her chalkboard. The opponent then tries to guess which number he or she wrote. If the opponent guesses incorrectly, the first player crosses out that number on the list and goes again with a new number. If the opponent guesses correctly, then it is now their turn to write a number. The first one to cross off all of the numbers on his or her list is the winner.

Tips: The player who starts first has an advantage, so players should alternate the starting order. If chalkboards are not available, you can play outdoors and use sidewalk chalk. In this case, you will need something to cover up each child's playing surface, since it must stay concealed until an opponent takes a guess. Paper and pencil can also be used, but this makes it difficult to "listen to" the numbers as they are written.

ACTIVITY 110: Ten Prints

Objectives: Identification of a numeral and an amount, counting, correlation of a numeral with an amount, and artistic expression.

Materials for each child:
- thick tempera paint (add cornstarch to thicken paint)
- a plastic or styrofoam tray
- ten small similar stickers
- a popsicle stick
- a plastic lid

Procedure: Each child can dip popsicle sticks and plastic lids into paint to make number Ten Prints using the stick as the "1" and the lid as the "0." After making the prints on one page, offer more paper for them to create prints as they wish. When the Ten Prints are dry, offer each child ten stickers which he or she may choose to put on their artwork.

Tips: Depending on the developmental level of your children, you can experiment with printing several different numbers. Pipe cleaners bent in the shapes of different numbers can be given to the children to dip in paint, or you could ask them to make as many numbers as possible from zero to ten with just the popsicle stick and lid. (0, 1, 4, 7, 8, and 10)

ACTIVITY 111: Baby Ben Puppet

Objectives: Numeral identification.

Materials:
- 3" pieces of ribbon
- 1/2" x 1/4" piece of white paper
- construction paper
- scraps of foil
- scraps of tan or brown tissue paper
- markers
- scissors
- glue

Preparation: Draw or photocopy a number ten in blocked form onto a piece of construction paper and cut it out. Glue a piece of tissue paper to the top of the number one to make it resemble the nipple of a baby bottle. Next, make a face for Baby Ben on the number zero. Draw features and glue on a paper tooth, ribbon hair, and foil tears. If you do not have ribbon, cut thin strips of construction paper and curl them using a blade of scissors. The one and zero can be glued to popsicle sticks. Allow these to dry before the children play with them.

Procedure: Use this puppet in your number ten activities and with Activity 112.

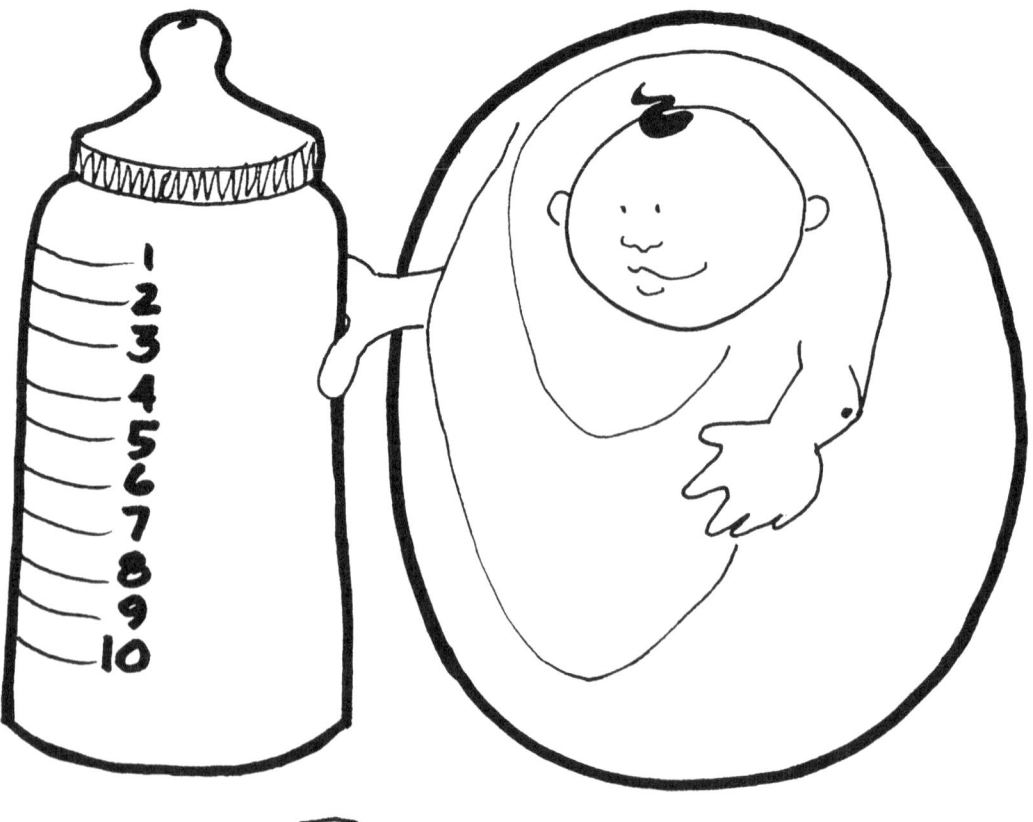

ACTIVITY 112: Baby Ben - A Puppet Song

Objectives: Numeral identification, and music and rhythm skills.

Baby Ben

Chorus:
Ten, ten, Baby Ben, ten, Baby Ben,
Baby Ben and his bottle look just like a ten.
Ten, ten, Baby Ben, ten, Baby Ben,
When he cries for his bottle now and then.

Baby Ben is too small to talk and say, "Hi," so
When he wants his bottle, he lets out a cry.
There goes that loud, "Waaa-a-a!" from Baby Ben,
Now he and his bottle look like a number ten.

Tips: During the verse, separate the one and zero until Baby Ben cries for his bottle.

Ask the Children: What number does Baby Ben look like? What number does his bottle look like? What is zero plus one? (One.) When you put the numerals together, what do you get? (Ten.)

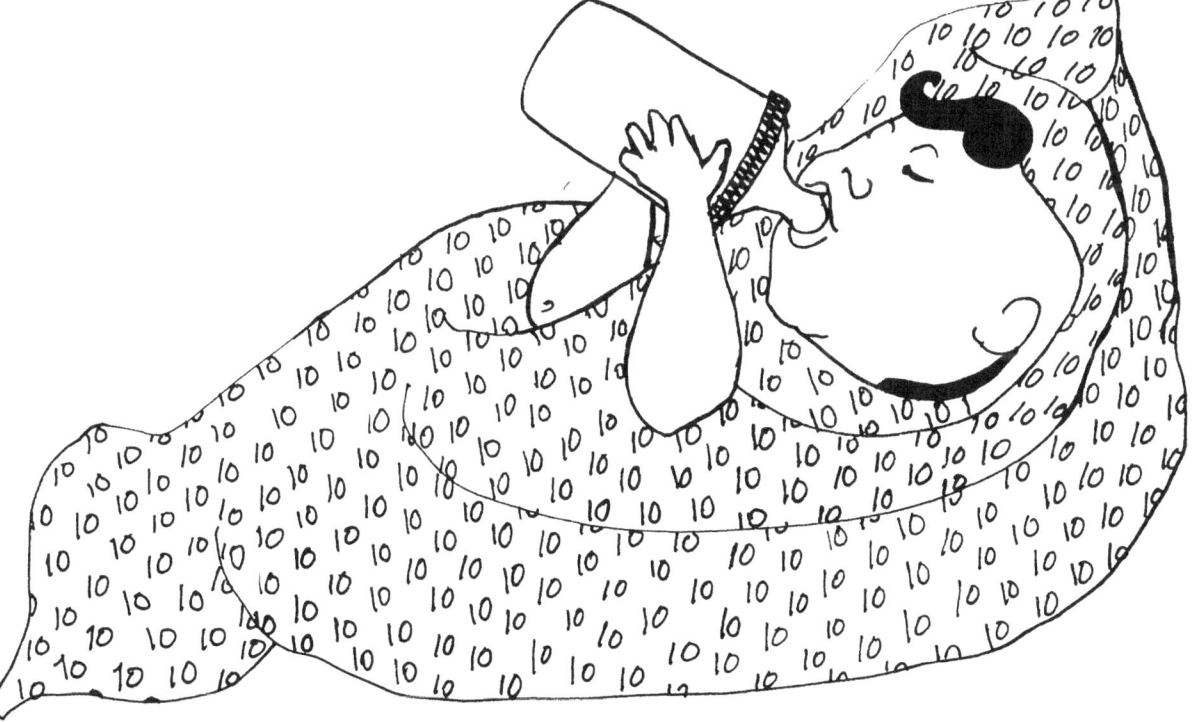

ACTIVITY 113: Ten Finger Prints Art

Objectives: Numeral writing, identification of an amount, correlation of a numeral with an amount, fine motor skills, and artistic expression.

Materials:
- large pieces of white paper
- tempera paint or ink stamp pads
- markers and crayons
- small bowls of soapy water
- towels

Procedure: Have the children dip their fingertips in the paint or stamp pads. Then tell them to press their fingertips onto their papers. After they have made their prints, have them place their fingers into bowls of soapy water to wash them, and then dry them. Allow the fingerprint pictures to dry. Then give the children markers or crayons to make their fingerprints into pictures. The prints could become apples, lady bugs, fish, balloons, flowers, or part of a design. Allow the children to use their own creative ideas.

Ask the Children: How many fingers do you have? How many are on each hand? What is five plus five? If you draw a one in front of a fingerprint, what number does it resemble?

Tips: Many print shops give away white roll end paper for free. If you can, look in your telephone directory for local print shops and ask if they have this and other art materials you could use with your children.

ACTIVITY 114: Number Ten Necklaces

Objectives: Identification of a numeral and an amount, addition, counting, and fine motor skills.

Materials for each child:
- ten 2" straw sections
- ten paper cupcake liners
- a 25" piece of yarn
- markers
- a hole punch

Preparation: Take several plastic drinking straws and cut them into 2" pieces. Cut enough to make ten pieces for each child. Poke or punch a hole in the center of each cupcake liner. For each piece of yarn, wrap one end in tape for easy threading and tie a knot in the other end.

Procedure: Tell the children to number their cupcake liners from one to ten with a marker. For younger children, draw the numbers with dots and allow them to connect the dots to make the numbers. Have the children thread their yarn through a cut straw piece, and then through the cupcake liner marked "one." Then they can add another straw piece and the number two cupcake liner, continuing until they have threaded all ten of the straws and cupcake liners. Tie the ends of the children's necklaces together so they can wear them.

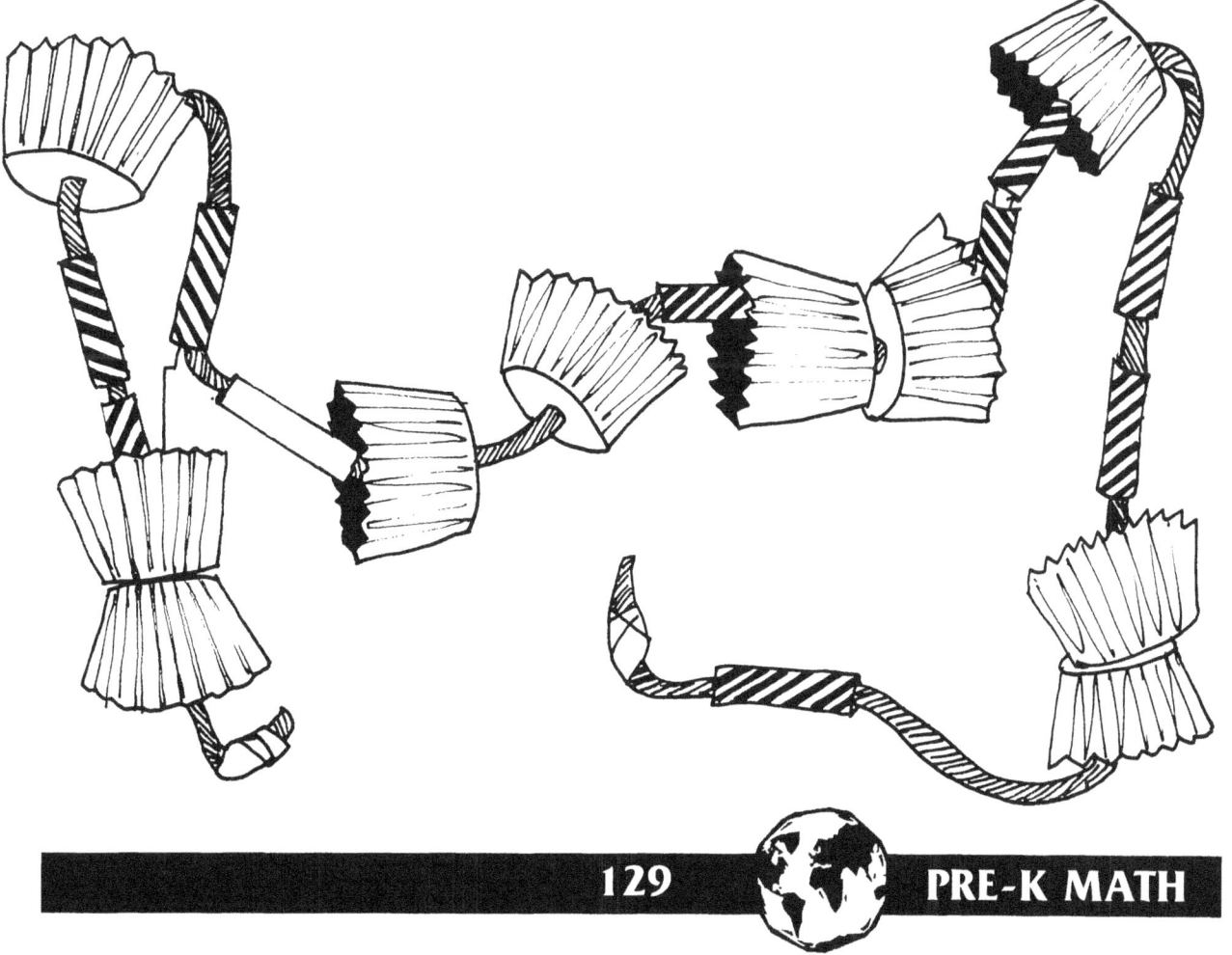

ACTIVITY 115: Number Ten Cash Register

Objectives: Counting, identification of a numeral, differentiating amounts, and correlation of numerals with amounts.

Materials:
- sharp scissors for the teacher
- a permanent marker for the teacher
- 54 juice or milk container lids (See the following reproducible parent letter)
- a large shoe box with a lid (available free from many shoe stores)
- a 5" x 6" polyfoam sponge
- glue

Preparation: To make the cash register, glue the sponge to the top of the shoe box lid. Use sharp scissors to cut ten slots in the top of the box lid, also cutting through the sponge. Label each slot from one to ten, writing on the sponge with the permanent marker. Cut a flap in the front of the box, which the children can use as a drawer to reach into and remove the play money. To make your own coin currency, use the permanent marker to write a "1" on one of the lids, a "2" on two of the lids, etc., until you have reached "10." Paper money can be made by cutting up used envelopes, or paper to be recycled.

Procedure: The children can play store and take turns being the cashier. The shoppers can even wear hip wallets to carry their play money. Please see the following activity for how to make these. Have several pretend products or small items which the children can purchase from you, such as stickers, snacks, or have a movie that the children must pay to watch. Let them count out the change to you.

Tips: For the polyfoam sponge, check with local carpet dealers for free scraps of carpet pad, or it is always available for sale at fabric stores.

LETTER TO PARENTS

Date:

Dear Parents:

Please save your lids from milk containers and soda or juice bottles for us, we will be needing them for an upcoming learning activity. Please wash them in the silverware rack of the dishwasher, or with soap and hot water. We will be using several lids and caps in an activity which calls for play currency. This activity will teach the children about counting coins, addition, subtraction, and estimating amounts.

I greatly appreciate your continued help and involvement!

Sincerely,

ACTIVITY 116: Hip Wallets

Objectives: Counting, estimation, and differentiating amounts.

Materials:
- old envelopes
- yarn
- a hole punch

Preparation: Give each child an envelope, preferable a used one, with a hole punched in each side. Let them thread a piece of yarn through each hole, and tie the envelopes around their waists.

Procedure: As you play the cashier, give each child a different number of coins and bills to keep in their hip wallets. Have them estimate how much you have given them, and then count it out with them, so they know how much they have. Encourage the children to count out their coins and play with their money in dramatic play.

ACTIVITY 117: I Can Count to Ten in French - A Song

Objectives: Counting, learning words from the French language, music and rhythm skills.

I Can Count to Ten in French

Chorus:
Uhn, deuh, twah,
CATre, sank,
seese, set, weet, nuff, deese.
Uhn, deuh, twah,
CATre, sank,
seese, set, weet, nuff, deese.

I can count to ten in French.
Now, won't you try it with me?
I can count to ten in French.
Now, won't you try it with me? *(To Chorus)*

You can count to ten in French.
I'm proud of you and me!
You can count to ten in French.
I'm proud of you and me! *(To Chorus)*

Tips: Practice the chorus slowly, line by line at first. The following are the correct spellings for the numbers one through ten in French. You may have success with pronunciation and accent if you rent a French film, or borrow a French language tape and let the children listen for just a few minutes. Exposing the children to various foreign languages and other cultures at this impressionable age will lay the foundations for a lifetime of curiosity. Please check the Appendix for several multicultural resources recommended especially for the early childhood classroom.

one: *un* (uhn) the "n" sound is made in the back of the tongue
two: *deux* (deuh)
three: *trois* (twah)
four: *quatre* (CATreh)
five: *cinq* (sank)

six: *six* (seese)
seven: *sept* (set)
eight: *huit* (weet)
nine: *neuf* (nuff)
ten: *dix* (deese)

ACTIVITY 118: Tour de Preschool

Objectives: Numerical value of time, visual identification of numerals, counting, and gross motor skills.

Materials:
- several big wheel bikes or tricycles
- a tablet of paper and pen to record times
- a piece of paper for each child
- stickers, or other small rewards
- masking tape or safety pins
- a stopwatch
- a marker

Preparation: Use paper and markers to make a number to pin onto each child's shirt. Find a safe location for your race, free from any traffic or obstacles. Establish start and finish lines, and determine how many laps the children will go around. Tell the children about the Tour de France, which is a worldwide bicycle competition held in France every year. This race is routed through both the city and countryside. Race participants don't even stop riding to eat or drink, they are followed by motor vehicles which provide them with food, medical, supplies, and other necessities.

Procedure: Have two or three children race at a time, and record their times. The object is not to compete and try to "beat" each other. Tell them that you will be writing down their times on a piece of paper. Reward them each with equal applause and a sticker.

Graphing the Results: Either on the chalkboard, or using a large sheet of paper, a marker, and a yard stick, make a graph with the children's names across the top and the times by 5's down the left column. Have each child find his or her name and time, and then find the point where they meet. Or, you could place an "X" at the child's coordinate, and he or she can simply shade in the section.

UNIT TWELVE
Backward Counting

ACTIVITY 119: Yakan Top (yahKAHN tope) - A Game from Turkey

Objectives: Subtraction, backward counting, addition, and fine motor skills.

Materials:
- a soft foam ball
- a large, open, outdoor space

Preparation: Divide the players into two teams, which will be denoted as Team A and Team B. The teams can pick their own names. Divide Team A in half and have them line up facing each other about ten feet apart. Team B will stand in the middle.

Procedure: The players on Team A are to throw the ball at the Team B players. When a Team B player is hit, he or she is dismissed from play. When Team B has only one player remaining, Team A has ten chances to hit that player. If Team A does not succeed, then all of the Team B players return to the center of the field, and Team B scores a point. If Team A succeeds in hitting the last player, then no points are scored, and the playing positions are reversed. The game continues up to a predetermined score.

Bonus Lives: If someone on Team B catches the ball in mid-air, he or she receives a bonus life. If hit with a ball later, he or she may give up the bonus life and remain on the field. If Team B accumulates more than ten bonus lives, then Team B automatically scores a point, and all of the Team B players return to the field. If Team B is down to one player and has bonus lives remaining, then Team A must take away all bonus lives before having the ten final throws. During these final throws, catching the ball is not allowed.

Tips: If you think the children are capable of throwing a ball hard enough to cause pain, consider making your own safe gameball by tying rags or old clothes together. Make sure there are no zippers, buttons, etc.

ACTIVITY 120: Rockets

Objectives: Backward counting, numeral identification, and scientific exploration.

Materials:
- paper towel tubes
- construction paper
- scissors
- masking tape
- markers
- star stickers

Procedure: The children can design and decorate their own rockets. You may wish to ask them if they would like help with writing the numbers from ten to zero down the side. Rent a video, or borrow books from the library to show the children rockets blasting off and simulate the countdown with their homemade rockets. Use these rockets in dramatic play and with the movement game in Activity 121.

Tips: You can take this opportunity to introduce the children to space exploration. Young children are fascinated with rocketships and other planets. In the Appendix you will find *Science, Air, & Space,* an activity book which focuses on early learning of these concepts and more.

ACTIVITY 121: Rockets, Blast Off! - A Movement Game

Objectives: Backward counting, motor and rhythm skills, scientific exploration.

Rockets Blast Off!

Let's count down!
(Hold up all ten fingers)

Ten, nine, eight, seven, six, five, four, three, two, one, zero!
(Put one finger down at a time)

Blast off!
*(Form hands into the shape of a nose cone
on a rocket, and move hands upward)*

Tips: This can also be done with the children pretending that they are the rockets. They can squat down until the blast off and then jump up into the air. Or, have them stand up straight in the beginning, and squat down lower and lower with each number until they are ready to spring up again when you hit zero. For more ideas which link movement and poems or songs, consult the Appendix for information on the book, *Drama & Music: Creative Activities for Young Children.*

ACTIVITY 122: Ten Special Children Dolls

Objectives: Addition, subtraction, counting forward and backward, visual identification of amounts, and appreciation for cultural diversity.

Materials:
- ten wooden clothespins (non-hinged)
- a shoe box
- acrylic paints
- paint brushes

Preparation: Place the clothespins on the edge of the shoe box. Paint faces with skin of different colors on each doll. Mixing brown and white paints together makes many varying skin shades. Vary the hair colors and eye colors, as well. Paint clothes, arms, and legs on the dolls and allow them to dry.

Procedure: As you read the poem in the following activity, add another doll to the shoe box edge. As you start to count backwards, remove one doll at a time. Allow the children to use these in their playtime, or for more counting activities.

PRE-K MATH

ACTIVITY 123: Ten Special Children - A Fingerplay

Objectives: Backward and forward counting, identification of amounts, correlation of numerals with amounts, rhythm skills, and appreciation for cultural diversity.

Ten Special Children

One, two, three, special children,

Four, five, six, special children,

Seven, eight, nine, special children,

Ten very special kids,
That's you!

Ten, nine, eight special children,
Seven, six, five special children,
Four, three, two special children,
One very special child,
That's me!

Tips: Have the children count forward and backward with their fingers as you add and take away the ten special children dolls.

ACTIVITY 124: Thermometer

Materials:
- a real plastic thermometer
- sharp scissors for the teacher
- red construction paper
- a black marker
- posterboard
- putty adhesive

Preparation: Draw a thermometer on posterboard and write the numbers from zero to ten with the ten at the top and the zero at the bottom. Draw a line across the thermometer to mark the location of each number. Cut a horizontal slit at the bottom of the thermometer and color a red circle under the slit. Cut a long strip of red construction paper to be your thermometer's mercury. Insert the red construction paper mercury from the back through the slit at the bottom, and place a small amount of putty adhesive at the top. As you pull the construction paper through, you can change the "temperature" reading on the thermometer.

Procedure: You can post this in the room and adjust it each day depending on the weather. Show the children a real thermometer and tell them what it measures. Use the thermometer in your counting unit and with Activity 125.

Tips: After using the thermometer, you can adjust the readings to use it for different things. For example, label the thermometer from bottom to top with "Silence," "Quiet," "Normal," "Loud," and "Noisy." When the children are being too loud, just go over to your thermometer and adjust the mercury until they quiet down.

ACTIVITY 125: My Thermometer

Objectives: Backward counting, numeral identification, and rhythm and motor skills.

My Thermometer

My thermometer says it's getting very cold,
Getting very cold, getting very cold. *(Hug shoulders)*
My thermometer says it's getting very cold.
I can see the red go down.

Ten, nine, eight, seven, six, five, four, three, two, one, zero,
Br-r-r-r-r-r! *(Shiver and chatter teeth)*

Tips: This can be just a hand motion or fingerplay activity, or a movement song. The children can crouch down very low as the red goes down, and jump back up and say "Br-r-r-r-r-r!"

ACTIVITY 126: Peacock Perception

Objectives: Numerical sequencing, number recognition, and correlation of a numeral with an amount.

Materials:
- peacock and feather pattern
- bright, multicolored sheets of paper
- scissors
- putty adhesive
- markers

Preparation: Use the pattern to photocopy the peacock's body and cut it out. Do the same with the feathers, or make feathers any size you wish, using very bright paper of several different colors. Use a marker to write the numbers from zero to ten, one number on each feather. Use putty adhesive to attach the peacock's body to a wall. Place pieces of putty adhesive on the back of each paper feather.

Procedure: Shuffle the paper feathers. The children can sequence the feathers and place them in the correct numerical order on the peacock's back. For less advanced children, make two feathers for each numeral. Attach one set of feathers to the peacock's back in the right order. Then the children can use the other set of paper feathers to match them with the numbers already attached to the peacock, placing each corresponding feather on top of the one already attached.

Tips: To preserve this activity for future use, you may wish to have it laminated, or use felt pieces for use on a flannel board. You can write different letters, chores, children's names, etc., on the feathers instead of numbers.

Pattern for Peacock Feathers

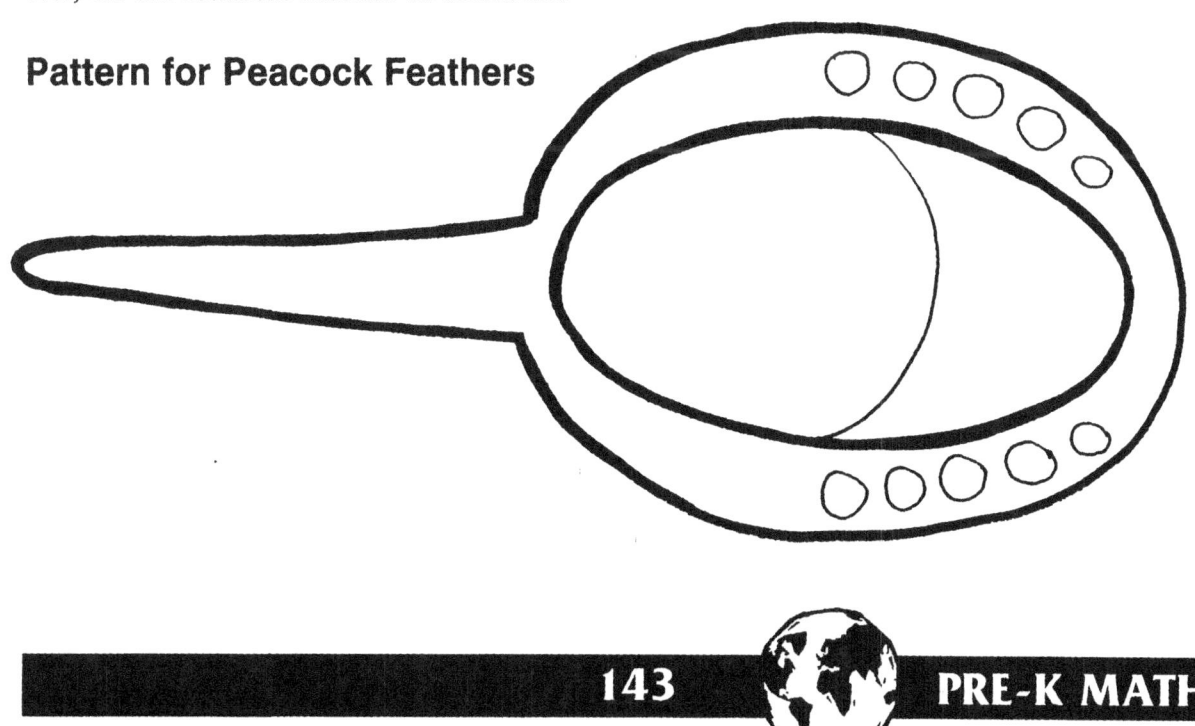

Pattern for Peacock Body

ACTIVITY 127: A Measuring Turkey Baster

Objectives: Addition, subtraction, visual identification of amounts and volumes, and forward and backward counting.

Materials:
- a turkey baster
- a permanent marker
- food coloring

Preparation: Make ten evenly spaced horizontal lines from the top to the bottom of the turkey baster. Number each line from one to ten with one being at the bottom and ten at the top.

Procedure: Allow the children to use the turkey baster with colored water (add a few drops of food coloring to water) during water play. They can see firsthand how two important math principles work as they watch water move into (addition) and out of (subtraction) the turkey baster.

Tips: You might want to set up a science table for the children, including the Measuring Turkey Baster and several containers for them to pour and mix with. Do not use food colored water or anything that will stain when letting the children play freely, since spills are inevitable.

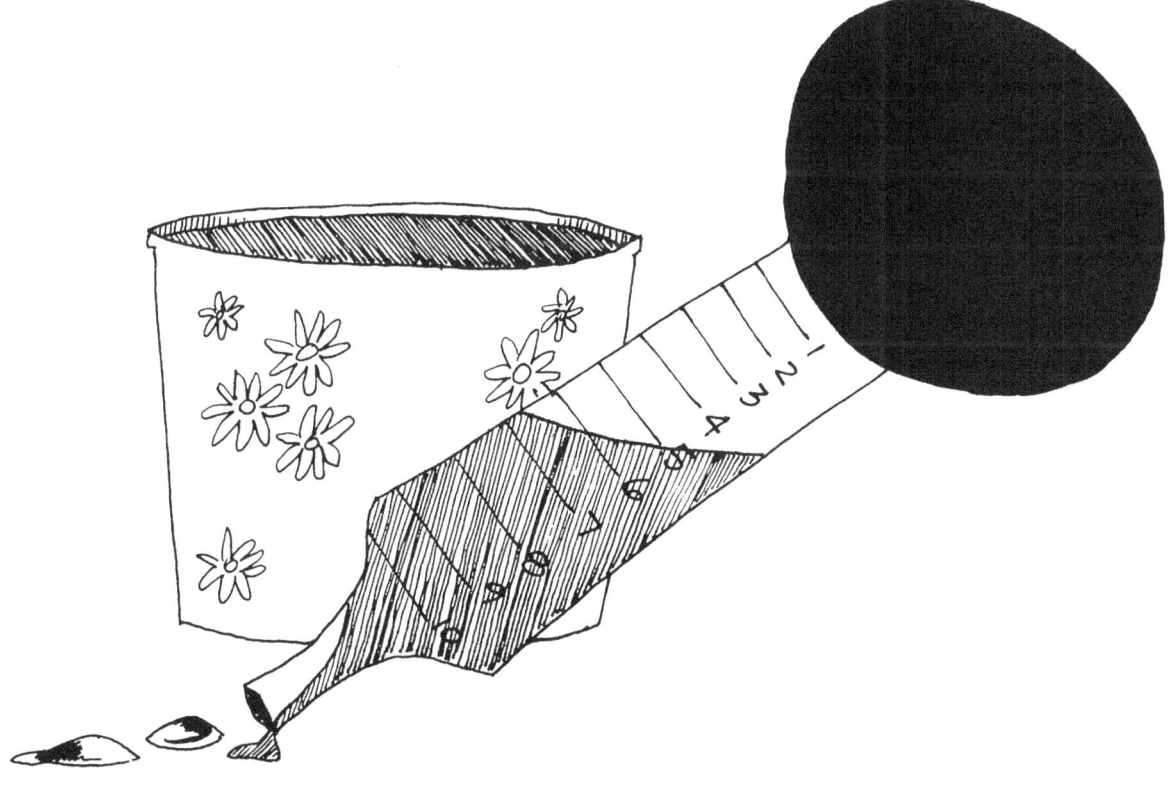

ACTIVITY 128: Numbers Incline Board

Objectives: Addition, subtraction, and forward and backward counting.

Materials:
- a lightweight board
- a long strip of paper
- various objects which roll
- small toy cars
- tape

Preparation: Obtain a long board, such as a lightweight sheet of paneling, dry wall, or something similar to a balance beam. Make sure that there are no rough edges or sharp corners for the children to hurt themselves on. Tape a long strip of paper onto the board and number it from zero to ten. Prop one end of the board up about 2" off the floor, and let the children roll objects down.

Procedure: Instruct the children not to climb on the board when it is propped up on an incline. Allow the children to roll cars down the board, round objects, anything which slides. Let them experiment with different textures and weights to see which slides faster. Run a car slowly down and count the numbers as they go by with the children. They can have races with the cars and different objects.

Tips: Leave the board flat on the floor when you have finished. The children can still slide different items along like shuffleboard, or walk on the numbers for fun.

ACTIVITY 129: Tornado Tube

Objectives: Subtraction, addition, science concepts, and empty/full.

Materials:
- a Tornado Tube
- an hourglass
- two empty 2-liter soda bottles
- a permanent marker

Preparation: Locate and purchase a Tornado Tube. Use the permanent marker to write the numbers ten to zero on one bottle and zero to ten on the other bottle. Fill the bottles with colored water as instructed in the Tornado Tube directions.

Procedure: The children can tip the Tornado Tube toy over and watch the water level, moving to a lower number in the top bottle and reaching a higher number in the bottom bottle. An hour glass, or a salt-filled egg timer can also be overturned, so the children can watch the same process with sand.

Tips: Tornado Tube is a device which attaches between two plastic soda bottles. It causes the phenomenon of a natural tornado to occur within the top bottle. Please see the Appendix for how to obtain one of these. Also listed in the Appendix are two books which are similar to the Tornado Tube in subject matter. These books, *Hurricanes* and *Earthquakes* introduce young children to science and weather concepts at a very simple level while maintaining interest.

ACTIVITY 130: Hopping on a Caterpillar

Objectives: Counting forward and backward, and numeral recognition.

Materials:
- six inexpensive vinyl placemats
- sharp scissors for the teacher
- a permanent marker
- a large plastic lid

Preparation: Use a pen to draw around a plastic lid while placing it on a vinyl placemat. Use sharp scissors to cut out twelve circles. Save the excess scraps to use for making other items for your children. Place the glossy sides down and use the permanent marker to write the numbers from zero to ten, one on each circle. Draw a face and antennae to make the head on one of the circles. Draw many little lines at the bottom of each circle for legs.

Procedure: The children can line up the caterpillar's body in numerical order and hop from one number to the next. They can invent many games and ways of using this toy. After you have finished, consider taping the circles to various spots in the room either on the floor or on the walls, to indicate different areas. For example, if you want to tell a story, and you have taped circle seven to the rug in the corner, tell the children, "If everyone goes and stands by the seven, you'll get a big surprise!"

Tips: Shoes with rubber bottoms should be worn if the vinyl placemats have a glossy finish. Socks can be very slippery and should not be worn while hopping on these.

ACTIVITY 131: Stairs

Objectives: Counting forward and backward, and self-esteem.

Materials:
- plastic or wooden building blocks

Procedure: Make a stack of ten blocks, then a stack of nine blocks, then eight, etc., until you have only one block. Put these stacks together, making stairs to use for counting and playing. Have the children line up by height in one long row. Starting at the shortest end, assign each child a number. Then, one by one have them call out their numbers both forward and backward. Take each child out of the line separately, so they can see the "human stairs" they make.

Ask the Children: Is one person better than another because of their height? Tell the children that just like the stairs, every height is needed to make the group complete. Every stair is essential, special, and important, just like every height.

Be a Child When You See a Child

Be a child when you see a child.
Cherish every day.
Help a child,
Guide a child,
Enjoy them while they play.

Love a child,
Support a child,
Marvel as they grow.
Kiss a child,
Hug a child,
Your love through them will flow.

Cynthia M. Manthey

APPENDIX

Activity 1
Vaughn, Gloria Ed.S. and Frances S. Taylor M.A. *The Flannelboard Storybook.* Atlanta, GA: Humanics Learning, 1986.

Activity 30
Drawing by Elizabeth Lauersdorf, a 10-year old Korean American.

Activity 52
The Heritage Key, Inc. Catalog. 6102 E. Mescal, Scottsdale, AZ 85254. (602) 483-3313. An inexpensive Yut game imported from Korea may be ordered from this international children's catalog which also contains many games, books, toys, dolls, and other wonderful items from many cultures.

Activity 68
Graham, Terry Lynne M.A. *Fingerplays & Rhymes for Always and Sometimes.* Atlanta, GA : Humanics Learning, 1984.

Activity 85
National Federation of the Blind. 1800 Johnson St., Baltimore, MD 21230. (410) 659-9314. Braille alphabet cards are available at a low cost with free shipping. Call to place credit card orders or send a check. The items listed below are also available from this address at no cost, provided by The National Organization of Parents of Blind Children. When you call, also request these free items:
- Braille Storybook Resource List
- A pamphlet, The Blind Child in a Regular Preschool
- Booklets of personal stories of blind individuals. These can be adapted for preschool level.

Riekehoff, Lottie. *The Joy of Signing.* Missouri: Gospel Publishing House, 1987.(800)641-4310. Call to place credit card orders, order #020520. Hardcover, 352 pages.

Activity 91
Newman, Al. *Fibber E. Frog.* Atlanta, GA: Humanics Ltd., 1993. Also in the series, *Grub E. Dog, Fraid E. Cat,* and *Giggle E. Goose.* Picture books for the very young child, teaching concepts such as the importance of the truth, listening to others, and trusting others.

Activity 121
Hodges-Caballero, Jane A., Ph.D. *Science, Air & Space: Folder Games for the Classroom.* Atlanta, GA : Humanics Learning, 1993.

Activity 122
Rubin, Janet and Margaret Merrion. *Drama and Music: Creative Activities for Young Children.* Atlanta, GA: Humanics Learning, 1995.

Activity 131

To obtain a Tornado Tube, contact your local school supply store and request that they order one for you if not in stock, or order by mail: School Tools, P.O. Box 870470, Stone Mountain, Georgia 30087-0012. (800)552-7867. Order #BUR 01.

Gold, Maria Ph.D. and Stephen Gold Ph.D. *Hurricanes. Earthquakes.*(Two separate titles) Atlanta, GA: Humanics Learning, 1992.

General Multicultural Resources

Acazar Records. P.O. Box 429, Waterbury, VT 05676. (800)541-9904. Call to place credit card orders or to receive a catalog. A sturdy, hardboard big-book children's atlas entitled *It's a Big, Big World* which includes a cassette is available.

Creative Thoughts & Surplus Stuff. (800)886-6428. Call to place credit card orders or to receive a catalog. Multicultural modeling clay is available in four skin-tones, ask for item #632.

Hodges-Caballero, Jane, Ph.D. *Children Around the World: A Multicultural Journey.* Atlanta, GA: Humanics Learning, 1994. Games, recipes, crafts, and information on cultures around the world fill this revised and updated best seller.

Manthey, Cynthia M. With *Respect for Others: Activities for a Global Neighborhood.* Atlanta, GA: Humanics Learning, 1995. The primary theme companion to *Pre-K Math,* full of activities which build self-esteem, multiculturalism, and sensory awareness.

MCC Selfhelp Crafts. 500 Main Street, Akron, PA 17501. (717)859-4971. Contact to receive a retail catalog of handmade crafts and musical instruments from people in developing countries, including Mexico and some countries in Africa.

Multicultural Publishers' Exchange. (800)558-2110. Call to receive a free catalog of publications written by and about people of various races and cultures.

Multicultural Musical Cassettes

Learning Through Movement. 570 N. Arden Blvd., Los Angeles, CA 90004. (212)460-4387. Dance-a-Story, Sing-A-Song - Early Childhood Multicultural Cassette. A multicultural children's music cassette which contains an African game/song from Ghana, an African American call and response song, and music and stories from other countries. Includes lyrics and movement instructions.

Manana Para Los Ninos. P 1985 Machete Records, C 1989 EarthBeat! (A Division of Music for Little People), P.O. Box 1460, Redway, California 95560. Contact for a cassette of Mexican songs for children.

Music With Respect, Volumes 1 and 2. Quality Instructional Publications, Wisconsin: 1992. Call (608)837-4002 to place your order.

Ronstadt, Linda. Canciones de mi Padre. Elektra/Asylum Records: 1987. This cassette can be found in (or ordered by) the following record stores: Musicland, SamGoody, and Discount Records.

Related Resource Books

Commins, Elaine, M.Ed. *Early Childhood Activities: A Treasury of Ideas from Worldwide Sources.* Humanics Learning, Atlanta, 1982.

Knight, Michael, Ph.D. and Terry Graham, M.A. *Science Activities Pre-K through 3: Leaves are Falling in Rainbows.* Atlanta, GA: Humanics Learning, Atlanta, 1995.

Neuman, Susan, Ph.D. and Renee Panoff, Ph.D. *Exploring Feelings.* Atlanta, GA: Humanics Learning, Atlanta, 1983.

Rose, Angie, Ph.D. and Lynn Weiss, Ph.D. *Self-Esteem Activities: Giving Children From Birth to Six Freedom to Grow.* Atlanta, GA: Humanics Learning, Atlanta, 1994.

Trencher, Barbara R., M.S. *Child's Play: An Activities and Materials Handbook.* Atlanta, GA: Humanics Learning, Atlanta, 1991.

Whordley, Derek, Ph.D. and Rebecca J. Doster. *Humanics National Preschool Assessment Handbook.* Atlanta, GA: Humanics Learning, Atlanta, 1982.

ABOUT THE AUTHOR

For over ten years, Cynthia Manthey has taught preschool to children ages 2 to 5. She is a state Licensed Family Child Care Provider and currently acts as an Advisory Board Member for Project Team, "Together Everyone Accomplishes More," for her school district. Manthey also works as a part-time instructor in Early Childhood Education. She has had several articles on young children published and has conducted various workshops on topics such as self-esteem, positive discipline strategies, creative preschool curriculum, and multicultural preschool curriculum.

Manthey is also the author of *With Respect,* a companion book to this publication. Taking the same diverse, multicultural approach, *With Respect* gives teachers and parents the resources and tools to introduce different cultures to children at a preschool level. In the past, Manthey's talents for innovative teaching and music composition led to *Music With Respect,* a children's musical cassette published by Quality Instructional Publications in 1992. This cassette, full of original songs and rhymes, was created to accompany her first book, *With Respect,* a valuable preschool teaching resource.

www.ingramcontent.com/pod-product-compliance
Lightning Source LLC
Chambersburg PA
CBHW082123230426
43671CB00015B/2785